You, Too, Can Be Prosperous

Studies in Prosperity

by

Robert A. Russell

Martino Publishing
Mansfield Centre, CT
2013

Martino Publishing
P.O. Box 373,
Mansfield Centre, CT 06250 USA

ISBN 978-1-61427-469-8

© *2013 Martino Publishing*

Cover design by T. Matarazzo

Printed in the United States of America On 100% Acid-Free Paper

You, Too, Can Be Prosperous

Studies in Prosperity

by

Robert A. Russell

SHRINE OF THE HEALING PRESENCE
100 Colorado Boulevard
Denver, Colorado

To my good friends,
Edward and Greeta Landon,
whose enthusiasm, generosity, and vision
have been a constant inspiration,
this book
is affectionately dedicated.

CONTENTS

I

I

Am

Prosperity

Now lay this book down and repeat these words to yourself one hundred times. Repeat this practice at intervals until the words and their meaning become your basic thought pattern—an integral part of you. Read the book thoughtfully and meditatively in order to share the secrets of achieving prosperity that are revealed in these pages.

CHAPTER 1

THE PROSPERITY IDEA

"Where is the money coming from?" "How am I going to pay the rent?" "How am I going to get a new car?" "Why don't I get a better job?" "Why don't I get on faster?" "Why don't I get a decent salary?" "Why can't I be successful?" "Why don't I get ahead?" "Why am I always broke?"

Do you really want to know? Do you really want to do something about it? Do you really want to throw off the shackles of limitation and poverty? Then prepare yourself for one of the most thrilling and interesting experiments you have ever made.

When you picked up this book, you picked up one of the most important and valuable documents you have ever held in your hand. You picked up a practical and usable technique that has enriched and re-vitalized the lives of thousands. You picked up a formula that has abundantly demonstrated itself. You picked up a method of demonstration that will work for anyone who will put it into practice. You picked up an idea that can transform, change, and improve everything in your world.

If you followed the instructions on page II of this book and the mental soil was right, you started a vibration that will make all your dreams and wishes come true. You started a train of causation that will spread like wildfire until it touches every corner of your world. You started a flow of prosperity action that will drive every condition of penury, want, and lack from your life if it is not impeded by thoughts of an opposite character. You opened the door to the source of all achievement, wealth, power, success, discovery, invention, and material gain.

This idea is so big, so powerful, and so irresistible in its action that it will magnetize everything in your life and cause everything to vibrate in harmony with it. It will draw success, work, opportunities, and beneficial activities of every sort to you. Its vibration is so strong that it will demagnetize everything unlike itself. Its power is so great that it will penetrate and dispel every inharmonious condition. It spreads its light, its vitality, its riches to every part of your world. It is Omnipotent and Omniscient.

If you are lost in a maze of false beliefs, the idea will bring you to your goal. If you are in the poorhouse, it will take you out. If you are financially flat on your back, it will lift you up. If you have reached bottom, it will take you to the top. If your faith is weak, it will make you strong. If your attitude is right, it will accomplish all things through you. It will activate good—amplify power—increase income —attract opportunities—release riches—cancel debts—stimulate business—enlarge consciousness—prevent failure—strengthen faith—nourish aspiration—clarify vision—generate peace— heal disease—solve problems—increase ability— stimulate imagination—fulfill desires—recoup losses—remove barriers—eliminate hardships— release substance—dispel fear—neutralize worry —fire ambition—harmonize discord—destroy doubt—close gaps—intensify realization—integrate the mind—better conditions—purify judgment—substantiate claims—break fixation's —loosen tensions—open doors—penetrate appearances—reverse negatives: in short, it will realize the fulfillment of all your desires.

Prosperity! One single idea! Think of its power. Think of its far-reaching influence. The moment that idea begins to work for you, everything in your life begins to change. That moment, everything begins to improve. It is the key to your well-being. It is God breaking through to reveal to you the glories and riches of His Kingdom. Say over again: I AM PROS-PERITY! Millions slave for this idea; a few are supported by it. Do you see the difference? The laborer works for this idea; the capitalist lets it work for him. One supports it; the other is supported by it. Is there any difference then between the laborer and the capitalist? Only the difference in relationship. One is the servant of an idea, and the other is served by it.

Ideas are seeds that come to us from any-where and everywhere. They float through the air looking for the right mental soil. The right soil is a Consciousness of one kind, an unadulterated Consciousness in which there are no denials or contradictions. Just as vegetable seed to grow properly must have soil that is free of weeds, ideas in order to flourish must have soil that is free of contradictory and opposing thoughts. Our problem is not with the seed, as Jesus brought out in the Parable of the Sower, but with the soil. Remove the obstructions of fear, worry, and doubt, and the idea takes root and grows to maturity.

What is it you want—an apartment, a position, more money, or better health? Then drop your idea into the fertile medium of the subconscious. Plant it deep. Cultivate it with recognition. Fertilize it with concentration. Nourish it with faith, and activate it with your Consciousness. Condition your Consciousness, and there is nothing that you cannot have. *"All things are yours; and ye are Christ's; and Christ is God's."*

"If ye abide in me [that is, if you enter into and share my quality of Consciousness], *and my words* [my thoughts] *abide in you, ye shall ask what ye will, and it shall be done unto you."*

Do you believe this promise? Do you catch the impact of it? It means that our whole work is to keep our thoughts pure and our Consciousness true. If Divine Substance is momently shaping itself around our thoughts and materializing in our life the things about which we think, we must keep our minds off our troubles and keep them centered in God.

Now repeat the affirmation: I AM PROSPERITY. Say the words meaningfully. If you think prosperity all the time and keep every antagonistic thought out of your mind, prosperity is bound to be manifested in your life, for it *"abides"* in you, according to the promise.

"But how can I think prosperity all the time when there are so many other things to think about?" you ask. You can do it by making prosperity your basic or fundamental thought; that is, the master or primary thought from which all other thoughts take their color, tone, trend, and quality. Ralph Waldo Emerson said, "A man is what he thinks about all day long." The character of your objective thought will be determined by the primary or subjective trend of your thinking. The trend is the matrix or fixed mode through which all your other thoughts pass.

Worry usually begins in some small anxiety in the mind and becomes basic or habitual through repetition. We repeat the same worry day by day until it becomes a habit, or an automatic expression in our life. Habits make a path or channel through which our thoughts and actions travel. The channel enlarges as the thought is repeated and gets deeper and wider until the habit tends to dominate all our thoughts, actions, and character. That is why "A man is what he thinks about all day long."

If the basic thought of a man is worry, everything in his life will be tinctured by the progeny of worry—fear, timidity, uncertainty, depression, irresolution, doubt, bashfulness, indecisiveness, and lack of confidence.

The basic thought is much like a South African berry that the native holds in his mouth to sweeten everything he eats. Here is a man who has allowed worry to become his basic thought. This basic worry-thought will affect everything in this man's life. The whole brood of negative emotions will cluster close to it; others will sense his negative mental atmosphere and will be repulsed by it. No matter how good or how desirable his product or merchandise may be, as long as he carries this atmosphere with him, he will repel his good instead of attracting it. You have heard about the atmosphere of homes, buildings, towns, and communities that is made up of the collective thought of the people who live there, but the atmosphere of a man is what he "thinks about all day long." It is that subtle something that interprets him to others. If his basic thought is poverty or lack, others will know it and treat him accordingly.

How, then, shall we change these established

habits of thinking? By adopting new basic thoughts that will crystallize themselves into more productive convictions. Let this same man fill his mind with thoughts, assurances, and ideals of faith, with self-confidence, courage, and determination. Let him surround himself with an atmosphere of success, achievement, and power. Let him radiate qualities of fearlessness, trust, optimism, strength, and self-reliance. He will attract the best from everything and everybody. He will inspire confidence and compel attention. Believing in himself, he will inspire confidence in others. The new habit pattern will not only release the power of God into his Consciousness but will change the whole color, tone, and character of his life. Instead of worry, he will generate faith.

"But wait a minute," says a thoughtful student. "If you substitute one basic thought for another and make no disposition of the offending thought, you have two basic thoughts instead of one." That is true. "Then how will you keep from slipping back into the old basic thought of worry?" By tuning the old habit completely out, and by deliberately and persistently taking the new pattern of confidence and power into your conscious content.

The nature of habit is brought out clearly by Edward C. Beals in his booklet, *The Law of Financial Success.* "If you have to walk over a field or through a forest, you know how natural it is for you to choose the clearest path in preference to the less worn ones, and greatly in preference to stepping out across the field or through the woods and making a new path. And the line of mental action is precisely the same. It is movement along the lines of the least resistance—passage over the well-worn path. Habits are created by repetition and are formed in accordance to a natural law observable in all animate things and some would say in inanimate things as well. As an instance of the latter, it is pointed out that a piece of paper once folded in a certain manner will fold along the same lines next time. And all users of sewing machines, or other delicate pieces of mechanism, know that as a machine or instrument is once 'broken in' so will it tend to run thereafter. The same law is also observable in the case of musical instruments. Clothing or gloves form into creases according to the person using them, and these creases once formed will always be in effect, notwithstanding repeated pressings. Rivers and streams of water cut their course through the land and thereafter flow along the habit course. The law is in operation everywhere."

The way to eradicate the old process of worry is to form a bigger concept of confidence. As the confidence thought grows, the mental path of worry will gradually fill up from disuse. The old path will grow less and less distinct until it gradually disappears.

Do you see why this subject is so important? When you know how to change the basic thought, you know how to change everything in your life and are well on the way to something better and more productive of good. Remember, however, that Rome was not built in a day and that it is going to take time and patience to make new mental creases. The metaphysician calls this process *changing subjective trends*. You will see results when the new conviction becomes deeper and stronger than the old one. Once the new pattern is outlined and adopted, it must be repeated again and again with great conviction and feeling. You must make it the intimate, vital, predominating, ever-living quality of your thought. Say to yourself: I AM CONFIDENCE — I AM PROSPERITY — I AM POWER—I AM SUCCESS. Feel what you say. Feel it deeply and with great joy.

Dwell on your statements until they are firmly synchronized with your emotional nervous system.

There are several rules that will aid you in doing this:

1. Refuse to use the old habit path under any circumstances.

2. Keep your thought changed out of the negative path, and hold it in the positive.

3. Charge the new thought action with hope, power, belief, conviction, and determination when you express it.

4. Make your new pattern as clear, strong, deep, and positive as you can.

5. Make opportunities for traveling over this new path as often as possible.

The thing we want to accomplish is twofold: to obliterate the offending thought pattern, and to drop the new form into the pool of subconscious cerebration so that the new unimpeded idea can take form and substance. It is a process much like dropping a key or other metal object into a body of salt water. If you have ever been to Great Salt Lake, you have probably made this experiment yourself. You drop a metal key into the water, and after a time the salt will form itself in a perfect pattern around the key. Consciously or unconsciously, we must have a mental equivalent (pattern) of the thing desired, and in this case it is prosperity. The Law of Prosperity is already within our minds pressing to act. Our job is to release it for our daily needs—to open channels for its expression.

Let us think first about the mental equivalent in the process. (This is just another term for basic thought, pattern, or model.) Having examined and rid ourselves of all apparent opposition, we are now ready to synchronize the new model with the creative forces of the subconscious mind. We are ready to drop the key into the water, so to speak. *"The Spirit descended into the pool and troubled the waters, and a healing took place."* The object, of course, is to get the new idea out of your head (conscious content) and into the soul, or subconscious mind. The law does not work for the thing you want while you are holding your model in the upper or conscious mind; it works for fulfillment only when the idea holds you. St. Paul said, *"Let Christ* [the perfect idea] *be formed in you."* Let the idea form in you a Consciousnes of itself. Don't hold the idea, but let the idea hold you. Do you hear? That is very important. Do not affirm unless your affirmation is backed up with a corresponding emotion.

Many students fail because they do not understand this principle. We demonstrate our good by loosing it into the Law and not by parroting affirmation or mouthing decrees. The Law responds to us by corresponding to our states of mind; that is, it operates through our mental equivalents or beliefs. When the Principle of Prosperity is set in motion through affirmation and acceptance, the Law of Life operates through it.

Why must the new thought pattern be couched in the present tense? Why do we say, "I *AM* PROSPERITY" instead of saying, "I *SHALL BE PROSPEROUS"*? Why must we claim something we do not have? Life always works in the present tense by direct affirmation. Jesus declared, *"I AM* THIS," or *"I AM* THAT," or *"I AM* THE OTHER THING," and immediately the thing decreed began to take form according to Law. To say that we shall be prosperous is well and good, but we are putting our prosperity off until some future time. To affirm our good in the present is to cause it to appear. Law, plus acceptance, plus belief is the pattern. If the idea of prosperity is to become a power in our lives, we must inwardly accept it as a present fact. Our thought, will, imagination, and feeling must agree with what we say.

Now I am going to ask you to start building your basic thought for prosperity without further delay. Center your thought again in our affirmation: I AM PROSPERITY. This is the nucleus that is to grow and multiply indefinitely. It must be backed up with your earnest faith and desire. Your idea of prosperity may be a better position, more income, a nice vacation, an agreeable companion, or more health. It may be something you do not have but need desperately. The Law says that you can have anything you desire if you believe that you already have it; that is, if you have a subjective acceptance of the thing desired. Now contemplate that for a few moments—not the money to meet the mortgage, not the new car, not the new house but THE BASIC IDEA: I AM PROSPERITY. You are going to change your Consciousness out of the old mold of lack and into the new mold of plenty. You are going to create a new habit atmosphere and new thought inclinations. That is your big responsibility in the process. You are going to eradicate a mental equivalent of lack by substituting a mental equivalent of plenty. You are going to start this idea of Prosperity revolving on its axis at such a high rate of speed that it will draw into your life all the good things you need.

Now put the book down—close your eyes—relax—and repeat the affirmation slowly and with pointed purpose one hundred times. Take it easy, and feel your pattern deeply. Realize that with each repetition your new idea is going further and further underground until it is perfectly integrated with the Creative Mind. It now has the power to attract to itself all the elements that it needs for its fulfillment. The rest of the process is a matter of sustained attention, faith, feeling, acting, and seeing. See the new idea clearly. Realize it, feel it, and accept it. Speed it up with your belief. Keep it alive with your faith. Feed it with fresh, rich, powerful, and life-giving images. Give it motion through action. Act it out. I AM PROSPERITY. Realize how rich you are. Keep the prosperity ideas and thoughts circulating freely through your mind. See them generating abundance, opportunities, and success. Do not allow negative ideas to creep in and short-circuit your good. I AM PROSPERITY. Keep repeating it until it goes underground and takes form. I AM PROSPERITY. Feel it. Rejoice in it. Bless it. Love it. Speed up the rate of vibration by telling your subconscious mind that you are already prosperous.

If you want prosperity, don't say, "I want to get rid of poverty." Be affirmative and positive. Say what you mean, and mean what you say. If your thought is filled with the idea of getting rid of poverty, you are increasing poverty in your Consciousness. Your basic thought is abundance, opulence, plenty, and you are going to think and speak of nothing else. Oh, yes, I know, the rent is coming due and you have a lot of unpaid bills, but you are not going to think of those things now. You are going to think prosperity, know prosperity, feel prosperity and nothing else. You are going to etch prosperity so deeply in your mind that nothing else can come into your life.

That is what we mean by building a new mental equivalent. It is creating a new basic thought and impulsion that will flood your life with good. It is making a new path for God and then getting everything out of His way. It is taking everything in your Consciousness that is unlike perfection and trading it in for something better and more desirable. The problem is not with life but with the use you are making of it. If you would change your condition from poverty to prosperity, you must change your position in the law.

SEVEN DAY ASSIGNMENT

Are you ready for an assignment? Then here is what I want you to do. For the next seven days, I want you to work deliberately and with persistence on this one idea: I AM PROSPERITY. I want you to try to think of nothing else and to feel nothing else for that period of time. This doesn't mean that you will get your demonstration in seven days although it could happen right now. I want you to watch your attitude, thought, feeling, and conversation during that period of time to see that you do not once revert to your old way of thinking and feeling. Know what you want and declare it with such convincing tones that the subconscious will go right to work to materialize your desire.

Now, let us repeat the assignment. This week (beginning right now) you are going to take the idea, I AM PROSPERITY, and try to think of nothing else for seven days. If negative or contradictory thoughts creep in, catch yourself and refuse to entertain them. If that sinus or arthritis starts to bother you, if the job proves troublesome, if debt or the housing problem presses you, reject the thought. Say, "I am not going to think about illness—that job—those unpaid bills—that apartment. I am going to think only wealth and health. I AM PROSPERITY. This is the new thought pattern and habit of my life. It is the basic thought by which I test every other thought. I shall weave it so tightly into the fabric of my Consciousness that no thread of the old processes of poverty can find room."

I AM PROSPERITY. Say it over and over. Think of it. Dream it. Make it the intimate, powerful, and ever-living quality of your thought. Say to yourself: I AM PROSPERITY. I AM ABUNDANCE. I AM OPULENCE. I AM RICH. I AM SUCCESSFUL. Feel these new patterns—feel them earnestly, deeply, and convincingly. Feel them unceasingly. Thank God for them. Rejoice in them. Thrill to them. Let them sink deeply into your emotional nervous system.

If you are serious about changing the automatic expressions of your life, I want to give you a little suggestion that will help you. I have found the association method to be a great boon in establishing new habits, and I am sure you will, too. Take any article that you handle many times a day like your watch, pen, pencil, tooth brush, razor, knife, fork, spoon, drinking glass, towel, or key, and say every time you pick it up, "I am thinking of prosperity. I am thinking of plenty. I am thinking of abundance." You turn the key in the ignition of your automobile a dozen or more times a day. Use that act as an association process. Let it remind you that you are PROSPEROUS. Accept the reminder when you unlock the door of your home, when you open the safe, when you use the letter opener to open your mail, when you stamp your letters, when you spend money, when you put on your clothes, when you tie your tie, when you wash dishes, when you sew, when you sweep. If you will do this intelligently and systematically for a period of even seven days, you will be amazed at the beneficial changes and blessings that will come into your life.

CHAPTER 2

WHAT PROSPERITY IS

Few things are more sought after or more misunderstood than what Mr. Average Man calls prosperity. To a clerk in a store, a raise of five dollars a week is prosperity. To the wizard on Wall Street, a profit of a million dollars is prosperity. This great difference in response is possible because the value in which prosperity is defined is false.

Prosperity is not a matter of money. Ask any hundred persons you meet what their idea of prosperity is, and you will get a hundred different answers. What do they prove? They prove that prosperity is a state of well-being; it implies a free and easy access to all that is good and desirable, and connotes a free, complete, and satisfying life.

Riches come by the same law that metal objects come to a steel magnet. The power of attraction is not in the bar of steel but in the invisible force with which it is charged. So it is with supply. It comes not by hard work, physical effort, or will power, but by the Spirit of God embodied as a working force in Consciousness. This power draws material riches to one in abundant measure. They come not because of anything a person does on the outer plane but by virtue of his Consciousness, or what he is. *"For unto everyone that hath shall be given."* In other words, to him that hath the Consciousness of the Kingdom of God, *"all these things shall be added."*

We instinctively sense that these things are true, but we do not know how to become receptive. It is not the power of God's hand that is foreshortened but our realization of oneness with Him. When we get into a state of lack or want, it is so real to us that we cannot think of anything else. Our static and undisciplined thought perpetuates the lack. Jesus did not say that we were to become resigned to cramped and limiting conditions—poor homes, neighborhoods, clothes, and food; He constantly implied that we should have the best of everything. He demanded of the multitude, *"If ye . . . know how to give good gifts unto your children, how much more shall your Father which is in heaven give good things to them that ask Him?"*

Jesus clearly stated that His mission in the flesh was *"to bear witness unto the Truth."*

What Truth? The truth that ". . . *God shall supply all your need according to his riches in glory by Christ Jesus.*" The silver is His, and the gold is His, and "*the cattle upon a thousand hills*" are His. Moses admonished us to remember that it is the Lord "*that giveth . . . power to get wealth.*" As we delight ourselves in His law, whatever we do prospers. Depressions may come, banks may close, businesses may collapse, economic systems may change, but God does not fail. Why not? Because "*there is no power but of God.*" As long as Job thought about his troubles, his troubles grew; when he forgot his troubles and thought about God, his troubles flew, and "*Jehovah gave Job twice as much as he had before.*"

The universe is filled with God Substance, but it requires effort to convert it into supply. St. Paul said, "*I have planted, Apollos watered, but God gave the increase.*" The effort must be co-operative: man calls and God hears; man prays and God answers; man furnishes the pattern and God supplies the material. If we want a crop, we must cultivate the soil and plant the seed. If we want iron, silver, and gold, we must dig for them. So it is with the wealth of God's Kingdom.

Everything we need or desire is at hand, but we must resolve it into what we require. How do we transform the invisible Substance into visible wealth? By the cultivation and circulation of rich ideas. When we identify ourselves with rich ideas—ideas of wealth, opulence, affluence, prosperity, and plenty, we become channels fit to receive the outpouring of God's abundance.

Jesus said, *"Seek ye first the Kingdom of God and his righteousness, and all these things shall be added unto you."* In other words, we must shape our thoughts, desires, and aspirations to the Divine Pattern. Since prosperity is in the Divine Plan for us, it is our duty to express prosperity in every phase of our living. Since it is God's Will and Intention for us to be prosperous and successful, there must lie hidden in the soul the possibility of a greater experience —an infinite possibility that will remain inactive until we set it in motion.

If we have been in the habit of thinking of prosperity in terms of money or material possessions, we must change our thought. True prosperity, as referred to in the Bible, is not an end in itself but a means to greater freedom, increased livingness, and fuller expression of life.

It is related not to the number of things that a man owns but to the satisfaction he finds in the way he uses them, to the happiness he derives from them.

True prosperity is not measured in terms of palaces, servants, cars, chauffeurs, fur coats, and real estate, but in achievement, contentment, confidence, freedom, inspiration, beauty; in a clear conscience, abounding health and energy, rich thoughts, and deep awareness; in harmonious relations with others, love and devotion of friends, guidance in times of uncertainty, courage in the presence of fear, protection in the midst of danger, and peace of mind; and in the sense of joy that comes from the realization that God is instant and unfailing Supply.

If we are frank with ourselves, we have to admit that our chief concern has not been with the Kingdom of God but with the things of the world. Mary E. Turner says: "Our sense of values is wrong. This is due to our training. Mankind has put undue emphasis upon material blessings and has believed that they come only from material sources. We have thought that money was of the 'earth, earthy' and had no connection with God. Money is a manifestation of Substance; Substance is an attribute of Divine Mind, and to gain an adequate comprehension of the omnipresence of Substance is to acknowledge God as our sole provider. If we are not demonstrating as we should like, it is a warning that we should turn the force of our thought toward contemplation of the infinite riches of God. He showers them upon us when we open our mind to receive."

The dictionary defines *prosperity* as the "state of being prosperous; advance or gain in anything good or desirable; successful progress: attainment of the object desired." To prosper in this sense is to have access to everything where and when it is needed. It would enable one to face the future with the certain knowledge that whatever he needed would always be present when the need appeared. This is the kind of prosperity that Jesus had. It can be ours, too.

There are many reasons why we fail to attract what we want from life; the chief causes of failure are our limited capacities and our feeble expectations. We ask for inferior things when we might just as well have the best. We are like the woman who prayed that she might reach her uncle's bedside before he died instead of praying that her uncle might be healed. Or the young man who prayed for part of his tuition and got a third when he might have had it all. Or the minister who prayed all his life for just enough to meet his daily needs. God gave him what he asked for and no more. He never realized that he limited God's giving by his meager requests.

There is an important lesson here which we must not miss. If I need an automobile, why should I limit the response to a Ford when there are Cadillacs to be had? If I need a fur coat, why should I not ask for a mink instead of a muskrat? If I need a home, should I not ask for a new one instead of an old one? Jesus said, *"Hitherto ye have asked nothing in my name; ask, and ye shall receive, that your joy may be full."* He also promised that *". . . whatsoever ye shall ask in my name, that will I do, that my Father may be glorified in the Son. If ye shall ask any thing in my name, I will do it."*

When we ask for inferior or lesser things, we do so because our faith in God's promises is weak. If God is impersonal Law and "there is no great and no small," as Emerson said, it makes no difference to God whether we ask for the most expensive or the cheapest article. He gives one just as readily as He does the other.

Then where is the limitation in man's supply? It is in man's meager mental equivalents and in his lack of capacity to receive. He does not ask for the best because of his own limitations. He tends to think that material things are more important than spiritual things, and thereby shuts the best things out of his life.

What we need is not only a larger awareness of God's inexhaustible Substance but a capacity for acceptance commensurate with our claim. Our prayers must not only be definite but flexible. We should always expect something better than the particular thing for which we have prayed.

And now we come to something that must be said with great emphasis. The purpose of prayer in the realm of finances is not to ask God for a specific sum of money, a particular job, or a certain house, but for the purpose of opening Consciousness so that we may be able to comprehend and use the formless Substance that is all about us.

Since it is the nature of Consciousness to out-picture itself, the scientific and satisfactory way to bring out a new manifestation is to appropriate a new state of Consciousness. It is futile to tell a man steeped in poverty that he can be prosperous, but to give him the idea of entering a new state of Consciousness is to clarify for him the means of securing prosperity. Elisha, you remember, pyramided the widow's pot of oil until there was enough to pay all debts and to enable the widow and her children to live *"of the rest."* When we take our new understanding into the Father Consciousness, the Substance begins to move. The Invisible becomes visible; the command to ". . . *be born again"* is fulfilled.

Now let us ask a question: What is this greater prosperity? How does one realize it? The only prosperity worth having is God. He is the Source of *"every good and every perfect gift."* If we have Him, our prosperity is enduring and satisfying. If we do not have Him, our prosperity is fugitive, fleeting, and uncertain.

"The blessing of Jehovah maketh rich; and He addeth no sorrow thereto." The words of Solomon are true today. We must clear the channels through which Infinite Supply is to be stepped down into visibility by keeping God in the forefront of Consciousness. When our prosperity is the outgrowth of a rich Consciousness, it is satisfying, permanent, and secure.

Let us go back to the statement that God is the only prosperity worth having. What does it mean? Why do we say that God is man's all-sufficient prosperity in complete expression? We can make these statements with confidence, for God is the Source of all life, substance, form. If we build our finances on human strength rather than on the strength of God, on mortal wisdom rather than on Divine Wisdom, our prosperity will never be very great. We will never be really happy in our possessions because of a lurking fear that some one may take them from us. Failures and frustrations are the lot of those who believe that prosperity comes through man and can be lost through the same agent.

I like that word, *permanent*, because it reminds me of Heaven, God, Law, and all the spiritual things that never change. The source of permanent prosperity lies in our power to possess and to mold the Universal God Substance in our thought. There are many ways of doing this, but the simplest and most direct way is the one pointed out by Jesus: "*Whosoever . . . shall not doubt in his heart but shall believe that those things which he saith shall come to pass, he shall have whatsoever he saith.*"

Many well-meaning Truth students scout the idea of asking God for material things in the belief that this is a wrong use of prayer. This attitude has no foundation. One cannot separate God from His manifestations. It is right to pray for material things when we have the mental equivalent of them; in other words, when we have made ourselves worthy of them. Money in itself, on the other hand, is just as powerless as a stick of wood without the Consciousness back of it. The evil in money is the belief that it has power independent of God. The danger in material possessions is that when we possess them, they may turn and possess us. When we become slaves to them, we shut ourselves off from Heaven. When we relinquish our love of things, we can have them in abundant measure. *"What things soever ye desire, when ye pray, BELIEVE that ye receive them, and ye shall have them."* We know this intellectually; but when we are in need of money or other material necessities, we tend to look for them in the world of things.

Let us turn to the great affirmation in the Lord's Prayer: *"Thy Kingdom come. Thy will be done in earth, as it is in Heaven."* What are we asking for in this part of the prayer? We are asking that the invisible world of thoughts and the visible world of things become one. Heaven is a perfect state of harmony between the visible and the invisible. This harmony is not something that we *make* happen but something that we *let* happen. It is a new state of Consciousness. The Kingdom of God on earth and the Kingdom of God in Heaven are two ends of the same thing. Both belong to God, and both are controlled by Him.

The Kingdom includes our bodies, our health, our homes, our environment; our loved ones; our positions, our success, our incomes; our happiness, our interests—all the component elements of life and living. That is why Jesus said, *"Seek ye first the Kingdom of God . . . and all these things shall be added unto you."* When Heaven becomes really active in our minds and thoughts, all our needs will be met automatically. We shall no longer postpone our good, but we shall accept it in the present. *"Thy will be done in earth, as it is in Heaven."* These words mean that our good is here and now and that we are going to have it. God's Kingdom is a kingdom of the mind. It is within us; it is omnipresent. We can accept it or reject it. We can live in it or outside of it, but it is always there, awaiting our recognition, acceptance, and co-operation.

"To this end was I born and for this cause came I into the world that I should bear witness unto the truth." Ask yourself if you are bearing witness to a rich and loving God by accepting a small income, by living with doubt and worry, by scrimping and pinching, and by the devastating inability to make ends meet; in other words, by living with a *poor idea.* If it is the Father's good pleasure to give you the Kingdom of Heaven, isn't financial sufficiency included in its benefits? Doesn't it include attractive homes, automobiles, telephones, television, radios, fur coats, nourishing foods, education, travel, and all that you need to enable you to live a full, free, and opulent life?

". . . my God shall supply all your needs according to His riches." Do you believe this promise? Or do you still believe that to be poor in purse is to be rich in God? If your answer to the second question is *Yes,* you need to get better acquainted with Jesus Christ and His teachings. In His day, demonstrations of supply were an integral and accepted part of the Christian faith and practice. In poor districts and

without financial means, people demonstrated an abundance of whatever they needed to build their homes, finance their crops, and carry on their work. They knew the Law and used it. Their faith was so pure and simple that they asked directly for their need to be supplied and accepted the response in gratitude and humility. John prayed in this fashion for his disciple, Gaius: *"Beloved, I pray that in all things thou mayest prosper and be in health, even as thy soul prospereth."* Joseph, the Bible tells us, prospered because Jehovah was with him. Uzziah ruled Jerusalem for fifty-two years successfully. He was prosperous as long as he stayed with God; but when his contact with God was broken, his prosperity ceased. *"He shall bring it to pass."* The promise is made to those who commit their way unto the Lord (Law) and who *"trust also in Him."*

What are we trying to bring out? Simply these two truths: 1. Prosperity belongs to the righteous; 2. There can be no lasting prosperity apart from God.

Now let us ask again: What is this thing we call prosperity? Prosperity is wealth. What then is wealth? The word *wealth* is from an old Anglo-Saxon word that means weal. Your wealth is your weal; it is your good. It may be anything from a porterhouse steak to a sky-scraper. It may be a new car in your garage, a big balance in your bank, a yacht in the harbor, a turkey on the table, a fine wardrobe, or expensive jewelry. Your wealth is your good, or as Jesus said, your *bread*. *"Give us this day our daily bread."* Jesus in these words is not beseeching and imploring a reluctant God for food. He is saying simply, "All good is mine. It is that which I am. I accept it—daily bread, shelter, clothing, amusement, travel, education. *'All things that the Father hath are mine.'* I am taking what I need. It is my inheritance."

On another occasion, Jesus said, *"Blessed are the meek: for they shall inherit the earth."* The word *meek* is a misunderstood and almost obsolete word. Most people think of meekness as self-abasement or servility. They think of meek people as human door mats. Who could be proud of such a virtue? Such a virtue is a liability rather than an asset. What we need today are aggressive, self-assertive, two-fisted, big-muscled, heavy-handed men. *"Blessed are the meek: for they shall inherit the earth."* Pooh! What kind of talk is that? What chance has meekness in a world like this? Perhaps we should study again the lives of the mighty *meek* men in the Bible, and study in particular the lives of Moses and Jesus. Meekness is the virtue of which Jesus seemed to be most proud. *"Learn of me, for I am meek and lowly in heart,"* he said. The meekness he referred to is that quality of mind that keeps the Consciousness open to the good. A meek man is not a spineless creature but a strong man grown tender. The meek man is the gentle, patient, open-minded man who has entered upon his inheritance.

Do you hear today this Beatitude spoken on the mountain side so many years ago? *"Blessed are the meek: for they shall inherit the earth."* Jesus is calling you to let go and let God. Blessed is the man who lets go of his will, for he shall have the Will of God! Blessed is the man who lets go of John Doe, for he shall *"inherit the earth!"* The *earth* is symbolical of your possessions; it means position, income, food, clothing, and shelter. The meek *"inherit the earth,"* for they find in it peace, riches, and happiness that they make their own.

Your weal, then, is your prosperity. It signifies both material goods and well-being. Here you are, sitting in a universe of your own making. You are studying this book in the hope of improving that universe. How are you going to do it? By the multiplying power of Consciousness. In the same way that Jesus fed the five thousand. In the same way that He turned water into wine and filled the nets of the disciples with fish. Is your weal very small today? It can be increased if you will seek the Kingdom of Heaven first, and stop counting your prosperity in terms of dollars and cents.

Here is a student who had been out of work for eighteen months and who had asked for treatment for greater prosperity. He calls to say that he has been offered four very fine positions and that he now wants help in selecting the right one. Here is another whose demonstration of prosperity has resulted in his making money so fast that he must now become accustomed to a new security. A woman writes to say that her problem has been solved and that she is the happiest person in the world. Another now walks after a futile year of doctoring, heat treatments, baths, and massage. How do you account for these demonstrations? There is but one answer: *LIFE IS A STATE OF CONSCIOUSNESS.* As a man *"thinketh in his heart, so is he."* Change your Consciousness, and you change your world. Change your Consciousness, and you change your weal. The lack of Consciousness is the lack in purse, body, and world. Let's shout from the house tops so that every one can hear: *LIFE IS A STATE OF CONSCIOUSNESS!*

In the universe, there is but One Law—One Presence—One Power—One Substance. That Substance is Energy choosing to condense itself through your Consciousness. As one writer states it: "When you think of your money which is visible as something directly attached to an invisible source that is giving or withholding according to your thought, you have the key to all riches and lack."

What shall we say then of the one who seeks money for money's sake? There is but one thing we can say: he is mistaking the symbol for reality. It is true that we need money in the world we live in, for there is little we can do without it. Some one has said that money is "the concentrated essence of things desired, created, and established by society in its present stage of development." The important thing, on the other hand, is to keep it in the realm of symbols where it belongs. When we say that we need money, we mean that we need the things that money will buy. We need bread and

butter, meat and potatoes, and it takes money
to get them. Money can mean happiness, freedom, health, independence, contentment, peace
of mind, and the ability to help and to serve
others.

We pray, "Give us this day our daily bread."
But we are not asking for what belongs to another; we are asking for what is already ours.
It is a part of our inheritance. Our right to it
is implied in the word our, in the Father-and-
Son Consciousness in which the universe forms
itself and from which all things proceed. When
we say the words, Our Father, we recognize the
unity of all Life: the one Mind, Intelligence,
Substance, Power, and Source. We are no longer
in the world of John Doe; we are in a new di-
mension of Mind. It is ours by Divine Right,
and no one can take it from us.

What did Jesus mean when, on another occasion, he said, "Man does not live by bread
alone"? He meant that our life is more dependent on invisible forces than upon visible forces.
"The fact is," as E. V. Ingraham says, "that
most of the supply that we work for feeds only
two per cent of our nature. That which feeds
the other ninety-eight per cent is free for the
effort involved in receiving it. If this ninety-

eight per cent of our nature were habitually fed, the matter of taking care of the other two per cent would be simple and easy. Let us, therefore, try to consider supply in its broadest and fullest sense. Let us also be diligent in applying ourselves to every phase of supply in order that we may be most fully provided with all things needful. If we can feed some of the inner hungers first, we may find it a more simple matter to feed the remaining outer hungers."

Jesus said, "*I have meat to eat that ye know not of.*" He was not talking about physical food but about the food by which the mind, soul, and spirit of man are fed. We need bread on the table, but we also need the *"bread from Heaven."* We need the food that keeps the mind active and strong, the food that feeds our hopes, aspirations, and ideals. We need peace, harmony, grace, beauty, truth, and love. Yes, my friend, these are all a part of that greater prosperity which is in the Divine Plan for us.

Probably the greatest discovery of modern science is that all material things have their source in and are supported by an invisible and intangible substance called ether—the same ether that Jesus referred to as the Kingdom of

Heaven. Scientists are just now proving what he taught His followers more than nineteen hundred years ago. He was not describing an imaginary paradise up in the skies somewhere but was revealing to man the Source of Infinite Supply that is all around him. It is from this Kingdom, according to Jesus, that God feeds and clothes all His children.

"That is all very interesting," you say, "but what Scriptural authority do you have for such a claim?" Turn to the second verse of the 104th Psalm: *"Who coverest thyself with light as with a garment: who stretchest out the heavens like a curtain."* The word *curtain* in the Hebrew means a thin skin or film: and scientists tell us today that ether is so attenuated that a single cupful could encompass the earth.

If the properties of this vibrating fluid that fills all space and permeates everything are new and strange to you, let us use another illustration. What are man's two basic needs? Or better stated, what are man's two highest concepts of physical good? They are food and shelter. Food is everything on a man's table; it is everything to be found in the grocery, bakery, delicatessen, and butcher market. What is shelter? Shelter is the house, hotel, or apartment in which a man lives; it is the clothing he wears, the car he drives, and all the gadgets and devices that add comfort, convenience, and protection to his life.

Now let us resolve some of these things back into their native or basic elements. What is food? What are butter, milk, cream, and cheese? What are grapefruit, bananas, corn flakes, toast, and coffee? They are air, earth, and water— nothing more and nothing less. A house is made chiefly of bricks and lumber. What are bricks and lumber? Air, earth, and water. Nothing more and nothing less. What is a suit of clothes or a fur coat? Air, earth, and water. And what are air, earth, and water? They are universal properties through which God expresses himself in the physical world.

Let us return to a consideration of ether. The scientist tells us that it has no specific gravity. It is not derived from anything but permeates everything. It is the source of all life, power, vibration, heat, light, energy, attraction, gravitation, and repulsion. In short, it is the substance and form of every outer thing, including food, clothing, and shelter. St. Paul, in his letter to the Hebrews centuries ago, explained that *"What is seen hath not been made out of things which do appear."* All things are made out of this one Universal Substance which is God.

"All things that the Father hath are mine." Can you say these words now with conviction? Universal Mind Substance is instantly available and responsive to those who have learned how to lay hold upon it in Consciousnesss. It is always with us and always responds to our faith; it is not affected by our negative and depresssed states of mind, but is always in action, always awaiting our recognition and acceptance.

TEN THINGS TO REMEMBER
WHEN DEMONSTRATING PROSPERITY

1. The mental process necessary to a greater income is a matter of recognition, acceptance, and belief. This mental experience must precede any material manifestation.

2. Supply is fundamentally an invisible thing; it is the receiving into your Consciousness the Spirit of God, which created all things from the beginning and out of which all things are formed.

3. The metaphysical method for demonstrating prosperity is to put prosperous ideas to work.

4. Poverty is a state of mind. We bring about this manifestation by our negative recognition, acceptance, and belief.

5. We overcome poverty by mastering the sense of every kind of lack.

6. We look not to the world of things, persons, and places in solving a problem of supply but look within to our own Consciousness.

7. We master the sense of want by building an inner sense of plenty.

8. We can have anything we desire if we believe that we already have it.

9. Prosperity is not a matter of education, training, working, saving, investing, struggling, or denying yourself. It is a matter of getting into harmony with the Law of your own individual Consciousness and then following that Law to its logical conclusion.

10. The permanent source of our prosperity lies in our power to possess and to mold in our thought the Universal God Substance.

CHAPTER 3

THE SOURCE OF WEALTH

Where does all the money come from? Where do all the automobiles, diamond rings, houses, skyscrapers, farms, cattle, and horses come from? Where does everything come from? It all comes from the One, Primordial, Spiritual Substance out of which all things are created.

Our thoughts, our words, our bodies, our food, our clothes—everything that appears—are created from this Substance. It permeates everything, penetrates everything, and fills everything. It is the raw material of all forms. We think into it, and it gives back to us the results of our thinking. It is the invisible source of all Supply; it responds to our word. We contact it through the spiritual medium of our thoughts. It is Omnipresent, Eternal, Intelligent, and Encompassing. It thinks through our brains, materializes through our words, breathes through our lungs, feels through our emotions, speaks through our nerves, and repairs the worn-out tissues of our bodies. *"In Him* [Substance] *we live, and move, and have our being."*

"All things were made by Him [Substance] ; *and without Him* [Substance] *was not any thing made that was made."*

Substance is pregnant with life, intelligence, power, and healing. It is a Substance that thinks. When it engages vibration, it carries radio programs right into our homes. We do not have to take the roof off or put the windows up to let the radio programs in. They go right through cement, bricks, plaster, lumber, and steel without disturbing the structure in any way.

Thus we see the meaning of Omnipresence. There is nothing in the material world that is solid, impregnable, or impenetrable. Substance is in all, over all, through all, and under all. Substance will go through tons of solid rock or concrete just as easily as it will go through our bodies. We do not see, taste, feel, smell, or hear Substance, but we know it by what it does. When it engages man's thoughts, it materializes the thing imaged in the thought. It acts by means of belief and conviction. A prayer goes out into this intangible Substance and causes a vibration that changes the material conditions in a man's life. A declaration of healing moves right into the physical body and produces health. Then why are there so much poverty and sickness in the world? Because we direct this Substance toward negative and inharmonious ends. We do it by doubt, fear, anger, hurry, hatred, arrogance, vanity, and resentment.

Substance has been here from the beginning, but man is just now learning how to use it for his good. We all have access to this Substance, but it responds to those who recognize it and make use of God's Laws. Substance is not affected by our ignorance, limitation, and poverty.

Perhaps we should make a distinction here between Substance and matter. There is a difference, and to confuse them is to shut off our supply. When we say that God is Substance, we mean that He is the essence, or that which stands under or behind things—that which gives them being, reality, and support (*sub-stare* —that which stands under). *"Faith is the substance of things hoped for, the evidence of things not seen."* Contemplate these things, and you will see that matter is formed, but God is formless although He is the basis of all form.

Go on to the subject of demonstration, and you will see that creation is always like the thing imaged in the thought. *"Prove me now herewith, saith the Lord of hosts, if I will not open you the windows of heaven, and pour you out a blessing that there shall not be room enough to receive it."* We prove our dominion over material things and conditions by looking to the Principle behind them. If Substance responds to man's thoughts, he can direct it to the fulfillment of his needs. Do you get the feeling and promise of that? Do you see the possibilities? It makes no difference how hard times may be, the man who lays hold of Substance in his Consciousness will, as the Bible says, *"have plenty of silver."* He may lose a fine position today, but he will walk into a better one tomorrow.

Now just calm yourself, my friend. I am going to answer your question right away. The simplest and most direct way to lay hold of Spiritual Substance is the way Jesus suggested: *"Whosoever . . . shall not doubt in his heart* [subconscious mind], *but shall believe that those things which he saith cometh to pass; he shall have them."*

Do you understand that? The spiritual mediums by which you contact God are faith, thoughts, and words. In other words, you must put into your thoughts and words what you expect to take out of them. Good or not-so-good results are always like the thoughts that projected them.

Substance does not fluctuate with the stock market. It does not decrease with hard times nor increase with good times. It never runs out; it never becomes scarce. It is always the same—constant, generous, abundant, and free-flowing. Jesus referred to it as *"living bread"* and *"living water,"* and promised that he who feeds on God-Substance *"shall never hunger"* and *"shall never thirst."* Do you see what He was talking about? He was talking about a principle that is just as exact and immutable in its operation as the Law of Gravity. He was saying that you can no more be separated from your supply of Substance than the sunbeam can be separated from the sun.

Be frank with yourself. What have you been seeking these many years? Answer me. Have you been seeking the spirit of things or just things? Jesus said, *"Ye seek me after the loaves and fishes, and ye cannot find me."* Why not? What were you supposed to seek? You were supposed to seek the pure Substance of Spirit. You were supposed to worship the Cause instead of the effect. Then you did not hear the thrilling command: *"Ask, and ye shall receive that your joy may be full."* Not a quarter full nor half full, but *"pressed down and running over."*

Do you see now why Jesus said, *"Go and do thou likewise"?* Go, thou, and feed five thousand hungry men and women with two sardines and five biscuits. *"Go, and do thou likewise." "Greater things than these shall ye do."* Go, thou, and cast the net on the right side of the ship. Go, thou, and multiply the widow's oil. Go, thou, and heal the man sick of the palsy. Go, thou, and open the eyes of the blind. Go, thou, and still the storm.

Well, what are you waiting for? Why haven't you gone? I'll tell you why. You love things more than the Principle back of them. You have been content to read about Him and talk about Him. You have placed your hope upon things instead of placing it upon the fadeless Substance of Spirit. Things seem scarce, and you want to capture them before it is too late.

"O, ye of little faith," when will ye turn with your whole heart and mind? When will you take everything into your Consciousness and do your work there? How long will you

linger among the flesh pots of Egypt? *"Consider the lilies of the field."* Have you considered them? Look again. Not at the beauty, color, or perfume, but see *"how they grow."* No, it is not a waste of time to do this. It has to do with the money, home, job, car, and other things that you are trying to demonstrate. There is a lesson here; and if you miss it, you will miss everything. When you are told to consider the lilies, you are being told to consider the Power that brings them forth. There is a bulb (lily pattern) way down there in the earth; and as long as that bulb is there and undisturbed, it will bring forth an abundance of lilies.

Do you see the lesson Jesus is trying to teach? Do you see what He is trying to bring out? When you put things before God, it is like cutting flowers in your garden. They stay a few hours, and then you must get more. So it is with every thing on the material plane. Now, don't misunderstand me. It is right for you to gather lilies and share them with your friends. It is right for you to demonstrate money and spend it, but where do you go from there? Which is more desirable—the goose or the golden egg? Don't you see that when you go to the Cause behind money, you come upon a Power and Substance that cannot fail? Money is only as good as the government that makes it, but the Principle back of money is not dependent upon principalities.

"God so loved the world that He gave His only begotten son." He gave this Principle to you and to me and to every man. He gave it to us in order that we might be loving, happy, peaceful, successful, and prosperous. The Principle is always within reach, waiting to go into action, but it will remain inactive until we set it in motion through our thought. It is not money that is the root of all evil but the love of money. Money by and of itself has no power, but the love of money turns it to bad ends.

If you find this idea of Substance hard to follow, please turn to the chart at the beginning of this chapter. What do you see? You see money, a man, a house, an automobile, and food. Analyze these five objects, and you will see that they are all alike—that they are all made from the same stuff. The man, the money, the house, the automobile, and the food are all presentations of one element. And what is this element? What is this thing that makes them all

alike? What is their substance? The answer is
—paper. The only thing we have here is paper.
The man, the money, the house, the automobile,
and the food are but different forms made from
the same stuff—paper. The forms and the
paper are one and the same thing.

We call one form a man, another a house,
and another money, but they are all whatever
the paper is. The paper is a symbol of the Substance of which all things consist and out of
which all proceed. These pictured objects, then,
have no existence apart from the paper.

Have you been seeing things and praying for
things that are separate or apart from the paper
which is a symbol of Creative Substance? Can
you realize that you and the paper are one since
you are both the visible expression of Mind
Substance? And that apart from the Substance
you can do nothing, be nothing, have nothing?
Answer me. Of what benefit is all the Substance in the universe if your Consciousness
operates independently of it? Perhaps that is
what is wrong with your demonstrations. You
have been looking at things and disregarding the
power behind them. You have been seeking the
young man for the loaves and fishes and not for
spiritual understanding. Consequently, your

desires are still-born; you have prayers without answers, clouds without rain, forms without substance, and creations without life. When you withdraw your supporting thought, the creation falls apart and leaves you flat. Jesus said, *"Have faith in God."* Have faith in Universal Substance. Put rich ideas to work. Build for Eternity. *"Lay up for yourselves treasures in Heaven."*

What is this condition that has "stymied" you? Is it a belief in lack? Is it a fear of want? Then put your rich ideas to work as quickly as you can. Circulate them freely in this Mind Substance, and let them make you prosperous.

Stop calling attention to demonstrations that have already been made. Stop talking about the big deals you hope to put over, and give attention to the little ones now at hand. No one has any more power than you have, and no one is any closer to God than you are. It is true that Jesus did many mighty works, but they are not going to help you unless you contact the same Power he used. Summon your faith. *"Lay hold on life."* Say: "I have faith in the Substance of God working in and through me to increase and bring Substance into my world." Stop lamenting your shortages and losses. Stop limiting the Substance in your mind. There is plenty more where your former good came from. If Substance fills all space, there can be no lack of Substance anywhere but in your thought. It is not lack that needs to be overcome but your fear of lack.

Repeat your key affirmation: I AM PROSPERITY. How is this idea going to become substantial in your experience? By letting it form in you a Consciousness of itself. Know that you are in the very center of Creative Mind and that It is at work now producing the thing imaged in your thought. Thank God that He is at work on it now, bringing it into fulfillment. "Substance is plastic, and Spirit is compelling," said Spinoza long ago. The thing you desire is God wanting it through you. That is why you must lose your life before you can find it. *"I live; yet not I, but Christ liveth in me."* When Saul of Tarsus was dead, Paul the Apostle began to live.

Do you see what this does in the process? It shifts the burden of demonstration from your shoulders to God's. It removes personal responsibility and all other barriers that get in His way. Is your supply of money low? Is your purse empty? Then lay your hand upon it and bless it. Mentally count out a sum of money with your fingers, and see your concept filled with Substance ready to take form. Bless your food, your clothing, your car, everything you use and need with the thought of living Substance. Realize its Universal Nature.

"For he that hath [the Consciousness of Spiritual Substance], *to him shall be given: and he that hath not* [the Consciousness of Universal Substance], *from him shall be taken even that which he hath."* The more conscious you are of this Universal Substance, the more it will work for you, and the richer you will become. Have you ever noticed how some rich men hold their riches and become richer while others lose their wealth in a few years? The answer lies in the Consciousness of the men. One has a Consciousness of abiding Substance; the other does not.

"When we think that a substance is cold and dead," says Lowell Fillmore, "it becomes so to us. When we pronounce a blessing upon Substance, we quicken the life in it and it responds and begins to manifest the good from which it sprang.

"Metaphysical students are learning to bless

their money. They find by experience that blessing money increases prosperity. Sometimes this prosperity shows itself in a greater supply of money and sometimes the same amount of money seems to go farther. There is always an increase of good, an increase of buying power, for the one who blesses his money.

"To the average individual, money is cold cash. To one who understands truth, money becomes living Substance. Which do you think will be the best servant—for money is a servant—cold cash or living Substance? Do you not think that a living dollar will serve you better than a cold cash dollar? Some may think that is going pretty much into the realm of imagination. We admit that the imagination has to be called into action in order to attain this understanding, just as it has to be called into action in any creative work. All successful persons have had to use imagination to help them succeed. The difference between success and failure is often in the use that one makes of imagination. Imagination helps us to see in the dollar a willing, intelligent servant, while lack of imagination, or a negative use of it, leaves us with a cold, dead something that is worth only its face value and with which we can purchase very little."

Why was the woman healed who touched the hem of Jesus' garment? Because of the Spiritual Substance that filled His Mind and Body. There were hundreds of people who rubbed elbows with Him that day, but only one woman recognized the Substance and received it. She knew that if she could but touch His robe her physical need would be met. Do you get the impact of this miracle? Substance increases with use until it fills our whole Consciousness and manifests as abundance in all our affairs. *"Be still, and know that I am God."* Look to Substance. Recognize it. Put it through your thoughts. Claim it until it becomes your own. It will increase your prosperity, heal your body, solve your problems, and neutralize your fears.

THINGS TO REMEMBER ABOUT SUBSTANCE

1. Everything is made from the One Universal Substance.

2. Universal Substance is intelligent; it is a living, thinking Substance.

3. Universal Substance is activated through faith and thought. Thoughts impressed upon this thinking Substance produce the form of the thought.

4. Universal Substance is omnipresent. It permeates, penetrates, and interpenetrates all space.

5. The universe is friendly to your needs. God wants you to have all the Substance you can use.

6. When you start to demonstrate prosperity through metaphysical law, you must look to Substance and not to man. You must live and think in the opulent bounty and goodness of God.

7. Your point of contact with Substance is recognition. If you make no demands upon it, it will not manifest in your life.

8. What you receive from the universe will turn upon your belief that you already have it. You must think of everything you want in terms of actual present ownership.

9. Don't pray for more Substance but for a larger capacity.

10. Since there is no time but NOW, you must always act in the present.

11. When you make a claim on Universal Substance, have a well-defined mental picture of what you want. Vague, misty, and indefinite pictures do not accumulate Substance.

12. Never look at the visible supply; look always at the limitless riches in formless Substance, and know that they are coming to you as fast as you can receive and use them.

13. Think of this Substance as wax and of your thought as a die making an impression on the wax, and there you have the whole picture.

14. No depressions, hard times, panics, or unfavorable circumstances can defeat the man who looks to Substance for his supply.

15. If you would have the co-operation of your whole mind in what you are doing, never speak of your failures, losses, shortages, or limitations.

16. Riches that are secured by dishonesty and manipulation are dissipated by the same powers.

17. The thought that defeats Substance is the thought of competition. You do not have to envy, cheat, or take advantage of others because you are creating your own individual supply.

18. If you get money on a competitive basis, it is always subject to loss.

19. When you get money on the competitive plane, you take from others. When you get it on the Creative Plane, you give to others.

20. Remember that the thing you desire is God wanting it through you.

CHAPTER 4

THE MAGIC BOX

If you had a little Magic Box in your home that produced whatever you wanted whenever you opened the lid, what would happen to your state of consciousness, your thoughts, and your feelings? The first thing that would happen would be a complete change in your thinking. All fear would go out of it, all worry, all lack, and all sense of insecurity. Knowing that you could go to your little Box as often as you needed would eliminate all sense of limitation and strain from your mind. There would be no more poverty in your life. Having what you wanted when you wanted it would not only lift you above the plane of material need, but would (if the power were used wisely) make you a better, more useful, and more effective person.

Do I hear you say that this is all a lot of nonsense—a figment of the imagination? You are wrong. The Box is a symbol of your Consciousnesss, and to approach it in the right way, with the right idea in mind, is to cause the Box to open and to remove all want from your life. *"For all things are yours; and ye are Christ's;*

*and Christ is God's." "He that believeth on me,
the works that I do shall he do also; and
greater works than these shall he do."*

The principle of demonstrating prosperity is
as exact and unalterable as the principle of
algebra or arithmetic. There are certain laws
that govern the acquisition of riches; once these
laws are mastered and applied, riches follow
with mathematical certainty.

Perpetual prosperity is built upon three
things: recognition, acceptance, and sharing.
The greatest of these is sharing. Why? Because
sharing is the power that increases, multiplies,
and prospers. Some one has said, "Unshared
prosperity palls, and pines, and carries no blessing in it," and the Bible tells us, *"He that giveth
unto the poor shall not lack."*

We all want wealth in one form or another,
but financial wealth comes not through special
abilities, talents, thrift, influence, environment,
favorable conditions, or physical effort. It comes
as a result of thinking, acting, and believing in
a certain way; those who follow this way, consciously or unconsciously, purposefully or acci-
dentally, get definite results. Those who do
not follow this way remain in want.

It is not a matter of choosing a particular
locality, line of activity, business, profession, or
job. It is not a matter of living in Podunk,
Iceland, or Florida. It is not a matter of being
bright or dull, smart or stupid, strong or weak,
sickly or well. It is a matter of doing things
in a certain way and of holding to that way
through thick or thin. The potentiality of one
is the potentiality of all. If anybody has wealth,
you can have wealth; if anybody has a beautiful
home, you can have a beautiful home.

The Law of Supply is no respecter of persons. Since like produces like and since the Law
of Cause and Effect works in the same way for
all persons at all times, anybody who follows
the Law will infallibly demonstrate an abundant supply.

At the moment you may be the most disappointed, disheartened, discouraged, depressed,
and poverty-stricken person in the world; you
may not know which way to turn; you may be
without connections, prospects, opportunities,
and money; you may be flat on your back. But
if you begin to apply these principles and do
things after the Law, your whole situation will
begin to improve. If you need friends, you will
find them; if you need money, you will get it;

if you are in the wrong position, you will find
the right one; if you are in the wrong place,
you will find the right place. You can begin to
secure these results by starting right now where
you are to do things in the way that brings
success.

What is the way that works such miracles in
human life? It is the way of Consciousness.
Why Consciousness? Consciousness is your life,
the Creative Life of God. It is what you have,
where you are, how you work. It is what you
do, how you act, what comes to you, what
leaves you, the kind of friends and opportunities
you attract, and the kind of problems you have.
In fact, Consciousness is the determining factor
of every circumstance, experience, and condition
in your life; it decides whether you are successful
or unsuccessful, rich or poor, happy or sad,
strong or weak, peaceful or discordant, for all
are but the expression of your Consciousness of
the universe in which you live. *LIFE IS A
STATE OF CONSCIOUSNESS:* when we
have said that, we have said everything that can
possibly be said.

Now lean back in your chair, relax for a few
moments, and let me ask you a few questions:
What is troubling you at the moment? What

are you worrying about? Why are you fearful? Is it unemployment? Is it discord? Is it unhappiness? Is it lack of income? Then I say, *"Look to your Consciousness."* If you are suffering from lack in any form, it is because you are at this moment out-picturing what you have in your Consciousness. Are you hard-pressed financially? Are you out of work? Are you without a decent place in which to live? Then you are expressing in your objective experience exactly what you are holding within. Say this to yourself: "If thought is creative, then what I am and what I have at this particular moment simply image what I have in my Consciousness."

LIFE IS A STATE OF CONSCIOUSNESS. Write the words deeply in your heart. Lift the statement high in your mind. Without Consciousness, there would be no life. It comprises everything in your world. When you reduce everything in the universe to its lowest common denominator, you say, "I AM." You can never run away from yourself; you can never be other than yourself. When you express Consciousness, you use the words, I AM. You are told to work out your own salvation; no one else can think for you, and no one else can use your I AM.

Do you begin to see how the poor man becomes rich and how the sick man becomes well? Do you begin to understand what it means never to want again? St. Paul said, *"Be ye transformed by the renewing of your mind."* How does one renew his mind? By changing his thought. Then what is the way by which a man changes his bondage for freedom? He changes his thought and keeps it changed.

"Most men's Consciousness," says Thomas L. Masson, "is like an apple, in which the possibility of decay is always present, in which indeed, there are many soft spots; the problem is to keep it sound—not for any perverted or selfish purpose, but for the innate *priori* intuitive longing for oneness with God." Hold that for a moment and consider just how one is going to keep his Consciousness sound. Here is the possibility of decay (a soft spot). Let us say that it is the thought of bankruptcy or economic disaster.

How shall we restore soundness in the presence of such a weak and debilitating belief? By changing the thought out of it and by keeping it changed. Remember that a man always gets the things and conditions that belong to his Consciousness. If he has a Consciousness of money, he will get money; if he has a Consciousness of health, he will get health. The Bible tells us that a man is what he thinks in his heart. What he thinks in his heart (Consciousness) is what he attracts from life.

Isn't it perfectly obvious, therefore, that the way out of impoverished conditions is through a change in Consciousness? In fact, it is the only way you can change anything in your life. If you tell me that you are out of things or that you have a small salary, I say, *"Look to your Consciousness."* Put things right *there!* Find the offending thought or belief, and reverse it. Change your thought out of it, and keep it changed into something better. Speak the word with conviction and acceptance. Put into it what you expect to take out of it. Stay your mind upon it until it takes form. What do we mean by *the word?* We mean a clear-cut, definitely formulated thought.

"The word is creative," as Emmet Fox says, "and the strongest and most creative word is 'I AM.' Whenever you say 'I AM,' you are calling upon the Universe to do something for you, and it will do it. Whenever you say

'I AM,' you are drawing a check upon the Universe. It will be honored and cashed sooner or later, and the proceeds will go to you. If you say 'I am tired, sick, poor, fed up, disappointed, getting old,' then you are drawing checks for future trouble and limitation. When you say, 'I am divine Life, I am divine Truth, I am divine Freedom, I am divine Substance I am eternal Substance,' you are drawing a check on the bank of Heaven, and surely that check will be honored with health and plenty for you.

"Remember you don't have to use the actual grammatical form, 'I AM.' Every time you associate yourself in thought with anything or think of yourself as having anything, you are using a form of 'I AM.' The verb *to have* is a part of the verb *to be*. In the very ancient languages there is no verb *to have*. It is a modern improvement, like the radio or the automobile. *I have* means *I AM* because you always have what you are and you always do what you are."

Apply this principle to the affirmation, I AM PROSPERITY, and you will see how wealth comes out in your affairs. Whatever you believe becomes. Whatever you think expresses. You build your Consciousness with your I AM, by the things you think and do all day long. As a man thinketh in his I AM, so are his circumstances. Do you grasp that principle, you who are looking for better jobs, more income, greater freedom? If you do, the circumstances in your life will have to change. Did you ever stop to consider why it is that a man who has made a fortune and lost it can make another one faster than the man who never had one? It is because his Consciousness is greased in that direction. Do you know why many businesses disintegrate and fall apart when their founders die? It is because the supporting Consciousness has been taken away.

If we can show you what is wrong with your thinking, that knowledge should constitute the greater part of the cure for you. One of the reasons people fail to demonstrate sufficient income is that they imagine something other than God is their Source of Supply. Another reason is that they try to build prosperity without God. We cannot function from the Source (center) of Supply without Him. Those who do not undrestand this will try to change outer circumstances without changing their Consciousness—a process exactly like trying to lift one's self by one's own boot-straps. It is important to make up your mind about the things you wish to demonstrate, but it is more important to be willing to change your mind in order to get them. *"Of mine own self, I can do nothing." "The Father that dwelleth in me, He doeth the works."* The way is clear. The more you forget self and rely on God, the greater your demonstration will be. Metaphysics teaches you but one thing: How to be a good insulator through which the Power can flow. *"I, if I be lifted up from the earth, will draw all men* [manifestation] *unto Me."* When God (the I AM) is lifted up, your lack is turned into plenty. Do you begin to sense the riches that will be poured into your life when this adjustment has been made? *"My God shall supply all your needs according to His riches in glory by Christ Jesus,"* the promise reads. Your business is with God; nothing else matters. If you fail to receive the riches that are rightfully yours, it means that you are in God's way. There is some impediment in your thought that must be removed. Emerson told us to "Get our bloated nothingness out of the way of the

Divine circuits." Where the current is impeded, there is lack; where there is lack, there is a pinched supply.

What is the remedy for this condition? To repair the circuit and close the gap by filling the Consciousness with the thought of God. Now hold that for a moment, and consider this question: What does it mean to fill the Consciousness with the thought of God? It means to Practice the Presence for twenty-four hours a day. It means to keep Him in the forefront of your mind. *"I am God, and there is none else."* It means to know nothing but the Presence of God in every person, place, and thing. *"Power belongeth unto God."* It means to give Him all the power in your life. Power does not belong to disease, sickness, or lack; Power belongs to God. What is your definition of God? GOD IS ALL. God is thought and action. What God thinks becomes. To have an intimate contact with God is to have access to all His creations. "But I know that," you say, "and it doesn't work." If it doesn't work, you go about it in the wrong way. The right way is by REALIZATION. You must have a Consciousness large enough to appropriate the Supply that is already established in God for you. You must know and accept it with your whole mind. You are told to *"enlarge the place of thy tent* [your Consciousness].*"* If your Consciousness is small and picayune, you will have a small income and small success. You will experience smallness in every department of your life. You remember how St. Paul put it: *"Be not conformed to this world* [the world of the human mind—the world of small thoughts]: *but be ye transformed by the renewing* [changing] *of your mind." LIFE IS A STATE OF CONSCIOUSNESS.* All is mind. All is God. All is Universal Energy. *"This do, and thou shalt live." "This is the way, walk ye in it."*

Goethe, the German philosopher, said, "The highest and most excellent thing in man is formless, and we should guard against giving it shape in anything less than noble dress." This is just another way of saying that we have within ourselves the capacity to receive larger and richer gifts. Jesus expressed the same thought in this statement: *"Whatsoever* [all things] *ye shall bind on earth, shall be bound in Heaven: and whatsoever* [all things] *ye shall loose on earth shall be loosed in Heaven."* Heaven is the invisible realm of God's ideas. We use these ideas and give them form according

to our Consciousness and our application of
Truth. Let us not be discouraged when our
demonstrations have been delayed. *"Though
thy beginning was small, yet thy latter end
should greatly increase."*

Now we understand what Jesus meant when
He said to seek *"first the Kingdom of Heaven."*
The Greek word for Heaven is *Ouranos*, meaning expansion, enlargement, increase, multiplica-
tion, pushing-out. Seek ye first an enlargement
of Consciousness, and all things shall be added
unto you. Elevate your mind and multiply
your fruit. The Kingdom of Heaven is like
a grain of mustard seed that grows and expands
until it becomes the greatest among herbs. The
Kingdom of Heaven is like leaven that multiplies and expands until it leavens the whole
lump. How did Jesus feed the five thousand?
By the Law of Expansion. How did Elisha increase the widow's oil and save her sons? By
Expansion. Where is the Kingdom of Heaven?
Within. How does it expand? By recognition
and realization. To expand a balloon, you fill
it with air; to expand water, you apply heat:
to expand seed, you plant it in the earth; to
expand riches, you employ praise.

Charles Fillmore says: "There is an inherent

Law of Mind that we increase whatever we
PRAISE. The whole of creation responds to
praise. Animal trainers pet and reward their
charges with delicacies for acts of obedience;
children glow with joy and gladness when they
are praised. Even vegetation grows better for
those who love it. We can praise our own
ability, and the very brain cells will expand and
increase in capacity and intelligence when we
speak words of encouragement and appreciation
to them."

To praise will not only heal disease, remove
obstructions, and open prison doors, but will
cause veritable streams of riches to flow into
our lives. It will do things for us that we cannot do for ourselves. The quickest way to contact the Substance and Supply of God is through
praise. David in the Book of Praise (Psalms)
sang: *"Praise ye the Lord. O give thanks unto
the Lord; for he is good: for His mercy endureth
forever."* *"O that men would praise the Lord
for His goodness, and for His wonderful works
to the children of men! For He satisfieth the
longing soul, and filleth the hungry soul with
goodness."* *"I will praise thee, Lord, with my
whole heart."*

The central object of our praise, of course, is God, the Source of all our Good, and the act of praising should be a concomitant to everything in our lives. Was the breakfast good? Then say so. Did you have a good day at the office? Then say so. Acknowledge your blessings, and they increase. Praise God for what you have, and you will get more. Praise Him for what you do not have, and it will come to you. Bless your business, your employees, your customers, and your cash register. Bless every piece of money you receive. If you want a better job, bless the one you already have. If you do not have a job, thank God for the one He has for you. *"With thanksgiving, let your requests be made known unto God."* Thank Him for everything that seems to be lacking in your life, and it will be supplied. Bless your home, your family, your neighbors, your friends, your pets. *"Let all the people praise Thee. Then shall the earth yield her increase."*

"If anyone could tell you the shortest, surest way to all happiness and all perfection," wrote William Law, "He must tell you to make it a rule to thank and praise God for everything that happens to you. For it is certain that whatever seeming calamity happens to you, if you thank

and praise God for it, you turn it into a blessing. Could you, therefore, work miracles, you
could not do more for yourself than by this
thankful spirit; for it turns all that it touches
into happiness."

How, then, will you enlarge your Consciousness of Supply except by blessing and praising
what you have?

Review the chapter up to this point, and you
will see that we have stressed four things:

1. The importance of changing Consciousness.

2. The importance of keeping God in the forefront of Consciousness.

3. The importance of enlarging Consciousness.

4. The importance of praise.

This chapter is really a study of Consciousness. The study is of vital importance, for Consciousness is the medium through which everything enters or leaves your life. Prayer changes
things because it changes your Consciousness.
"It is done unto you according to your faith
[your mental equivalent, or scope of Conscious-
ness]." Jesus was not averse to our praying
for things that are in accord with God's pur-

pose. What He insisted upon was the acceptance and belief that we already have them in
our possession. Prayer must precede action.
Whatever is worth having is worth praying for.
Consciousness reaches its highest level in self-
forgetfulness.

The trouble with most people who get into
financial difficulties is that they become worried, fearful, and depressed. Their lack becomes
such an obsession that they cannot think of anything else. They do not realize that mental depression is the very thing that defeats them and
holds them in want. What shall we say to these
people? We shall tell them that the outcome of
their difficulties depends entirely on their attitude and trend of mind. If the mind can be
kept fifty-one per cent positive at such a time
(in the ascending tendency), their deliverance is
assured. The attitude or trend of mind is the
determining factor in every problem; it not only
determines how and which way the faculties of
the mind will work, but the speed with which
the need will be met. If the mental level is kept
above the fifty per cent mark, the mind will
work with the successful and prosperous side of
life. If it falls below, it will act with failure
and lack and will accentuate the difficulty.

How shall we raise the mental level at such a time? By changing our attitude and expecting the best from every person, place, and thing. Emerson said, "Assume a virtue if you have it not." That is good advice, and we can begin now by shifting the center of mental gravity from self to God, from the circumference to the hub. The first step is to make God the center of everything we say, think, feel, and do. This action will not only give the mind an upward and forward look, but it will raise the mental level.

The next step is to reverse every negative the instant it appears by giving all power to the Consciousness of Good. You will give no power to failure, delay, doubt, disappointment, despair, reverses, misfortune, or bad luck. What the mind makes, it can unmake. Do not get upset when things do not turn our right; do not expect the worst when things go wrong. Know that your mind has the power to make anything right. Refuse to be depressed or disappointed. Give no place to worry, fear, doubt, or uncertainty. When losses, misfortunes, and troubles come, meet them with the conviction that they are only temporary. If you are compelled to wait for your good, make sure that you are growing in the meantime. Do not let interruptions, recessions, or delays make you impatient. When you meet conflict or inharmony, refuse to become divided or distressed in your thought. Hold rigidly to St. Paul's statement, *"None of these things move me."* Look upon defeats, failures, and mistakes as putty in your hands. Maintain the attitudes and feelings that will awaken and bring out the best that is in you. Know that you can change circumstances and conditions by changing your Consciousness.

It makes no difference how poorly things may be going in the outer world, your job is to keep things going right in mind. The more you become conscious of in mind, the more your subconscious powers will produce for you. That is the Law of Increase. If you train your mind to think in terms of abundance, you will experience abundance in every department of your life. The things you desire will come to you in abundant measure.

Now let us recapitulate. Our purpose has been so to stock your mind with the ideas of abundance that they will cause your Consciousness to move in the direction of Abundance and produce for you those things which you specifically desire. It is important not only that you become aware of the fabulously rich powers of your mind, but that your desire for abundance be continuous and deep. There are millions of people who never get beyond moderate circumstances because they do not become conscious of the unlimited powers, potential possibilities, and vast riches in the mind. It is obvious that the larger part of their Consciousness functions independently of their good because there is no pattern to give it form.

The four important factors in demonstrating greater prosperity are these:

1. Remove every impediment and obstacle to the idea of prosperity.

2. Create a deep and continuous desire for abundance.

3. Become conscious of *more of everything* in your mind.

4. Use what you have.

The compensation will be large if you follow this pattern. Prosperity is wholly a matter of learning to make the most of what you are and have. The law says that you will receive more only if you use what you have. Use is the key that will unlock the doors of anything you want to do or accomplish. The rule is to have faith in yourself and to work with the Law.

"Son, thou are ever with me, and all that I have is thine." That knowledge is the Magic Box. We get worried and fearful, we turn to this person and that person, we consider this possibility and that possibility, and we get all worn out. And all the time, there is the Box—The Magic Box. What are we going to do with it?

"Every condition, every experience of life," says Robert Collier, "is the result of a mental attitude. We can do only what we think we can do. We can be only what we think we can be. We can have only what we think we can have. What we do, what we are, what we have, all depend upon what we think. We can never express anything that we do not first have in mind.

"The secret of all Power, all success, all riches, is in first thinking powerful thoughts, successful thoughts, thoughts of wealth and supply. We must build them in our own minds first."

"Could we rightly comprehend the mind of man," wrote Paracelsus in the Sixteenth Century, "nothing would be impossible to us upon the earth."

CHAPTER 5

GOD LOVES A PROSPEROUS MAN

"Our chief reason for claiming that God loves a prosperous man is that it is only as we experience good that God is expressed through us. The more completely we realize good—in all its manifold expressions, health, wealth, and happiness—the more completely do we express God; that is, the more does God become personified through us. So, God could have no knowledge of, or love for, the man who does not express abundance! This is a little hard to take, but if God could know anything of lack or limitation of any kind—lack of money, lack of health, lack of intelligence, lack of friends— then LACK would become an eternal verity, for God is changeless. What He knows today, He has always known, and will know throughout eternity. But God is always One—not a house divided against itself—and he can never know anything unlike Himself, so we need not be concerned about lack ever becoming a Reality."*

———
* Holmes, Ernest. *It's Up to You.*

"Where does all your money come from?"
is a question often asked of a minister friend of
mine. "You have so much more than other
men in your profession. You have a beautiful
home, Oriental rugs, and luxurious furniture.
You have the latest and most expensive automobiles. You wear the most expensive clothes.
Your church is flourishing, and you never beg.
You give generously to others and you have
plenty to spare," people often say to him.

Listen to his reply: "The Law of Attraction
is the reason for supply. *'Seek ye first the
Kingdom of God, and His righteousness; and
all these things shall be added unto you.'* Within
the law of the Kingdom is included the Law of
Supply. I do not look to salary checks, honor-
ariums, alms, and hand-outs for my supply. I
look to the formless Substance of God—the
same Substance that awaits every man who will
recognize it and use it, and to the Christ Within
who possesses all things."

"It took me years to get this understanding,"
says my friend, "and until I had it, I never got
anywhere with my finances. Like other men
in my profession, mine was a hand to mouth
existence, always in fear, always in debt, and
always in doubt. There is no reason why

every minister of the Gospel should not be as prosperous as the most affluent member of his congregation. It is just a matter of taking God at His word and proving Him."

It is one thing to lecture and preach about the bounty and opulence of God and quite another thing to activate it in one's life. This man was not rich to begin with, but he conditioned his mind to receive Divine gifts. He knew that if the Law was going to do anything for him, it would have to do it through him. What did Jesus mean when He said, *"The cattle on a thousand hills . . . . are mine"?* Was He talking specifically about livestock, cows, horses, and sheep? No, He was talking about everything in God's Kingdom. The expression, *"The cattle on a thousand hills,"* symbolizes everything on the material plane—money, houses, lands, jobs, food, clothing, automobiles, everything. These things are yours; they are mine. Christ told the disciples, *"It is the Father's good pleasure to give you the kingdom."* God gave *"the cattle on a thousand hills"* to us, and expects us to take them on His own terms. What are God's terms? The terms of faith, recognition, and acceptance. *"If I were an hungered, I would slay and eat."* The gifts of the Father are not ours until we recognize and accept them; when we recognize and accept them, we can have them. We can, as the Scriptures say, *"slay and eat."* But wait a minute! This is the point at which most people run into a snag. They go through all the metaphysical formulas and processes; they affirm God's abundance and the fulfillment of their desires. Then they beg and beseech God for that which is already theirs.

"We do more things to keep our prosperity away from us than we do to attract it to us," says Rhetta M. Chilcott. "If we did not, we should demonstrate more prosperity, for it is really more difficult to keep the good away than to attract it. But almost constantly we do things to put it out of our minds. We close our minds to prosperity; that is the reason why we are not prosperous. We pray for prosperity; then we tell ourselves that it is impossible to be prosperous. I know of no one who does not at times say: 'I cannot afford this or that.' It is not a good idea to say such things. If we recognize ourselves to be children of God, we can afford anything we desire. We are limiting ourselves when we say that we cannot afford a thing. We do not limit God—we could

not do that—but we limit our consciousness—
shut it up so that we cannot receive our supply.
I always think of it in this way: I set in action
the cause in the Unmanifest and then I bring
prosperity into manifestation."

Now hold that for a moment while we de-
fine the *Unmanifest*. The Unmanifest is the
Cause side of everything. It is the Christ Within
who possesses all things. If there is nothing
but God, and we are one with Him, and He
gives Himself to us freely, and He is everything,
then all things are ours. The first step in demonstrating an abundant supply is to know that
you are one with God and that consequently *"all
things are yours."* Yes, everything—money,
freedom, happiness, peace, health, wealth, and
abundance—more than you can ever ask or
think.

What is your situation right now? Are you
expressing debt instead of plenty? Then something is wrong. "You may," Miss Chilcott con-
tinues, "be pulling at the wrong end of the
purse string. Remember, you have hold of only
one end of that string. If you have hold of
the manifest end, you have hold of the wrong
end. You must hold to the Cause end, and that
is yourself—your Consciousness. You control

it absolutely. You control your finances whether you think you do or not. You control the amount that you get. It is absolutely up to you."

Let's get rid of the idea that we are the victims of circumstances. Poverty is not a verity but an idea of lack operating in our minds. It is our failure to comprehend and understand God. Since there is no lack in God, poverty can be changed. If we had a perfect Consciousness of the allness of God, we would automatically express prosperity in every department of our lives.

"The cattle on a thousand hills . . . . are mine." "The earth is the Lord's and the fulness thereof." "The silver is mine, and the gold is mine." It is not a far-off God who says these things to you; it is your own inner Christ who possesses all things. *"The cattle on a thousand hills"* are yours in the same way that the music that fills your house is yours. How do you take possession of that music and make it audible? By tuning into it. The tuning-in can be accomplished anywhere, at any time, and under any circumstances. So the man who recognizes God-Substance and provides the proper pattern for its manifestation will

know the truth of the statement: *"All things that the Father hath are mine."* He will *"slay and eat."* He will see opportunities, success, happiness, and supply flowing into him from every side.

How did Solomon become the richest man of his time? He developed the rich ideas that God had given him. Solomon was told that he could ask God for anything he desired. He could have asked for great wealth, power, or influence, but he chose wisdom, or rich ideas. His wealth came to him through the Queen of Sheba, the King of Tyre, and others who sought his help. Known as a man of great wisdom, he found riches flowing to him from every side. The metaphysician insists that rich ideas are the first requisite in demonstrating prosperity. If we recognize our spiritual inheritance and act with the Law, no good thing will be withheld from us. *"He that hath a bountiful eye shall be blessed."*

We all want an enduring and irrevocable prosperity; this kind of prosperity comes only through wisdom and understanding. It is not enough to affirm the truth; our understanding must carry with it an acceptance and a conviction. J. Lowrey Fendrich, Jr. says, "We cannot live the law by knowing it—we live the law by living it—and living it so profoundly as to be unable to escape a conviction of its eternal operation."

We activate prosperity in the same way that we activate health and power, and that is by the Law of Consciousness. Faith is the power of conviction. It is the power to know, to create, to formulate, and to achieve. *"The Law of the Lord is perfect."* How can we account for so many failures? In the same way that we account for so many successes. Both represent subjective trends in our thought. When a man admits that he is a failure, he must also admit that he is the maker of failure. Since there is no failure in the Divine Plan, failure is always self-made. The Universe is overflowing with abundance, but each man must fulfill his own destiny.

Emerson said: "Men suffer all their life long under the foolish superstition that they can be cheated." But it is as impossible for a man to be cheated by anyone but himself as for a thing to be and not be at the same time.

"When the impediment which is now obstructing the flow of your prosperity is removed, there will be an on-rush of blessings which nothing can resist," some one has said. The belief that others are cheating you constitutes a psychic block that inhibits any action of the Law of Prosperity.

Right now you are in the midst of a great reservoir of Spiritual Substance from which all things are made. It is subject to and responsive to your word. *"In Him we live, and move, and have our being."* *"All things were made by Him, and without Him was not anything made that was made."* What are you going to make out of this Substance? Yes, I am talking to you, you who are having such a difficult time financially. What kind of measure are you going to hold up to this reservoir of ALL Substance? How much are you going to take away? What kind of demands are you going to make upon it? How big is your mental equivalent? How comprehensive is your Consciousness? The reason God loves a prosperous man is because he manifests good in all its manifold expressions. How can you activate this Substance and express abundance? How can you bring it into your experience? There is but one way: *"Behold, I stand at the door and knock; if any man . . . open the door, I will come in to him and will sup with him."* Do

you hear? Did you notice that IF? It has
to do with opening the door. It has to do with
your conscious voluntary action. *"If any man
open the door."* Will you open it? Do you
know how to set the Law in motion? You
can open the door through your awareness that
God cannot know lack or poverty of any
kind. The force that activates Substance is
the Consciousness of the Allness of Good. If
you try to claim the cattle on a thousand hills
from the manifest side of life (without title),
you are likely to get into trouble with the
police. To gain legal possession of them, you
must appropriate them from the Unmanifest
side of life through the realization that we are
surrounded by a Substance that receives the
impress of our word and acts upon it creatively.

The people most troubled by finances are
the people who worship the dollar rather than
the power behind it. They are idolators, so to
speak, because they worship the coin (the
manifest symbol) instead of the source from
which it springs. Our government adopted the
inscription, "IN GOD WE TRUST", for our
money to remind us that God is the Cause and
supporting Principle of all form. Think what
it would do to our supply if every time we

received or paid out money, we made the affirmation: "In God We Trust." What a change in our affairs it would make! Now hold those four words for a few moments. Say them over to yourself, "In God We Trust." What does the affirmation do for you? It takes all responsibility for demonstration from your shoulders. It puts God first in your finances. It connects you with your Source.

Did you ever go to a mint and see how easily money is made? It is made just as automobiles, refrigerators, radios, clothing, and vacuum cleaners are made. Money is a symbol —an outward and visible sign of an inward and spiritual Substance. That is why we seek the Cause. *"The kingdom of God cometh not with observation: Neither shall they say, Lo here! or, lo there! for behold the kingdom of God is within you."* Do not look for that which is already yours. Release what you already possess into manifestation. The Cause is within yourself. "In God We Trust." *"And the Word was made flesh, and dwelt among us."* If you are working in the Unmanifest, you can be prepared for many surprises. *"With God all things are possible."* He will use any and all channels to bring your good to you. Nothing can hinder or impede its action.

The dictionary defines *trust* as "a reliance or practical resting of the mind on the integrity, veracity, justice, or other sound principle of another person, or upon his friendship, or upon his promises as involving these; faith." St. Paul has defined faith as *"the substance of things hoped for, the evidence of things not seen."* Do you understand that definition? It means that you must step out on the promises of God and dare to make your claim. Dare to claim His wealth and prosperity. Dare to penetrate appearances and acknowledge Him as your needed supply. Dare to trust Him and to lean on Him through thick or thin. You are told to keep your thought above the symbol at all times because *"Every good and every perfect gift is from above* [the Unmanifest], *and cometh down from the Father of lights, with whom is no variableness, neither shadow of turning."* Instead of thinking of currency, stocks, mortgages, and bonds, let us think, "In God We Trust." Instead of thinking, "I can't afford it," or "I am broke," let us think, "In God We Trust." Faith is both Substance and evidence, both Cause and effect.

MEDITATION

"The cattle on a thousand hills" are mine. The world is mine. The Universe is mine, for I am the child of God, free from all bondage. I am free. I am rich. I am power-full. I am one with all Good, and everything is mine to use. I claim my highest good now, and nothing can keep it from me.

CHAPTER 6

TUNING OUT

Does a country fly two flags at the same time? Does a man wear two suits of clothes at the same time? Can he think two thoughts at the same time? Can he do two things at the same time? Can he look in two directions at the same time? Can he see two sides of a coin at the same time? Can he follow two ideas and get one result? Jesus said, *"No man can serve two masters: for either he will hate the one, and love the other; or else he will hold to the one, and despise the other. Ye cannot serve God and mammon."*

Why do we persist in the double-sightedness that has produced so many paupers, failures, derelicts, misfits, parasites, incompetents, drifters, and beggars? Because we will not take the time to tune the mammon out of our lives. That is why St. Paul called us to self-examination: *"Examine yourselves, whether ye be in the faith; prove your own selves. Know ye not your own selves, how that Jesus Christ is in you, except ye be reprobates?"* Socrates said thousands of years ago, "The unexamined life is not fit for human living."

That is pretty strong language, but it is exactly what I am asking you to do in this lesson—to examine yourself. If you cannot be two selves at the same time, you must first decide which one you are going to be and then align the forces of your being with that side. You must cancel that which is death-dealing and magnify that which is life-giving.

All the Substance of the universe is around you. You can draw from it anything and everything you desire, but you must take the gift on God's terms. What are those terms? They are the terms of unity. Jesus said, *"If therefore thine eye be single* [if thy Consciousness be pure and one-pointed], *thy whole body shall be full of light."* The Substance must first go through you, not through John Doe and all the non-conductors of the human mind: the negative emotions such as fear, worry, anger, hate, and depression; such adverse conditions as unemployment, poverty, discord, illness, and loss of loved ones. When the word reaches you after such a detour, it is so weak that it is futile. The double-power doctrine has made it too feeble to take form.

The Chinese have a precept that says, "Not to correct our faults is to commit new ones."

Most of us want to correct our faults; but before we can do that, we must see that they are faults and recognize wherein we have fallen short. We must admit to ourselves that failure to be prosperous is the result of a lack within our selves. Let us examine ourselves to see what is wrong with our beliefs about prosperity. Since the basic magnet of opulence lies in our Consciousness, the fault must be in our thought. Somewhere along the line we have been sidetracked. We have taken a detour. We have strayed. What is it that we have forgotten? It is man's promised dominion over all the earth. We have accepted the belief that prosperity is something outside of us instead of something within us. The only thing that stands between us and our prosperity is a belief in two powers instead of one. When we can bring these two beliefs into perfect agreement, we shall have a steady stream of prosperity in our lives.

"Wherefore I put thee in remembrance that thou stir up the gift of God, which is in thee." One of the quickest ways to stimulate the flow of prosperity is to speed up your vibrations. Lift up your heart. Lift up your Consciousness. Stop looking for your prosperity to come

through a business, job, position, or profession. Realize that it comes through dwelling in a rich Consciousness. PROSPERITY IS. Your part is to accept it in mind and to thank God for it.

"But that is ridiculous," you say. "I work for Dorsey, Dorsey, and Dorsey," you say. "I am a paperhanger." "I am a lawyer." "I am a pharmacist." "I am a milk man." "I am a plumber." "I am a teacher, and my work is my source of supply. I depend upon the public through the School Board for my income." But according to Jesus, your Source of supply is God. All the money in the world belongs to Him, and He has said, *"I will never leave thee nor forsake thee."* Banks fail, corporations fail, jobs fail, professions fail, but God never fails. My friend, if your job were to play out tomorrow and you had an absolute realization of God as the Only Employer, you would quickly step into a better job than you had ever had before.

Often the trouble with beginners in metaphysical work is that they try to demonstrate their good while in a divided state of mind. They try to realize spiritual blessings in a Consciousness that separates itself from God.

Jesus stressed the importance of laborless activity, or living by indirection. *"I can of mine own self do nothing,"* said He; and later He said, *" . . . the Father that dwelleth in me, He doeth the works."*

When we live in conscious unity with God, the good begins to seek us. In order to get this sense of unity, the mind must be single. There are many references in the New Testament to the responsibility of man for clearing his mind of a belief in duality. *"Do men gather grapes of thorns or figs of thistles?"* asked Jesus.

In the parable of the sheep and the goats, you remember that the shepherd *"set the sheep on his right hand, but the goats on his left."* *"The Kingdom of Heaven,"* Jesus said on another occasion, *"is like unto a net, that was cast into the sea, and gathered of every kind; which, when it was filled, they drew up on the beach; and they sat down and gathered the good into vessels, but the bad they cast away."*

These parables compel a man to choose between the greater and the lesser. Until his decision is made, there will be no judgment, and conditions will remain unchanged. If you read these parables metaphysically, you will see that Jesus is talking about man's mind and his thought. He is compelling the individual to choose between the good (the life-giving thought) and the bad (the death-dealing thought). The realm of mind is like a net whereby the rich thoughts and the poor thoughts are brought to judgment and separated. The net is the mind; the fishes are man's thoughts; the vessel is man's Consciousness; and the sea is the one Substance in which they all function.

The divided mind catches every kind of thought. It is each man's responsibility to separate the good from the bad, the rich from the poor. In the modern radio, we find an apt comparison. What the listener hears depends upon his ability to tune out what he does not want to hear. The divided mind, as we said, catches every kind of thought. The single mind tunes out the bad thoughts lest the good thoughts lose their volume or be lost in the din. Such is the judgment which the clamorous horde of man's thoughts must face.

We have heard much in recent years about the return to prosperity, but there is no such thing. Prosperity is like health and peace. IT IS. What we are returning to is not prosperity but the consciousness of it. When we tune in to opulent and prosperous thoughts (that is, place them in the forefront of Consciousness) and tune out poverty and limited thoughts (that is, allow them to fall into inocuous desuetude), we shall discover that all things are ours.

Since two thoughts cannot occupy the mind at the same time, we cannot build a new Consciousness and new conditions until we have cleared a space for them by eliminating the old. Poverty thoughts must be tuned out before prosperity thoughts can go to work. That is why the Chinese say that "Not to correct our faults is to commit new ones." Thoughts are like magnets in our minds. They attract other thoughts like themselves. "Like attracts like" and "Like begets like" are old sayings based on experience. If we contemplate the idea of lack, we shall experience lack in many forms—lack of money, lack of peace, lack of health, lack of employment, lack of happiness, lack of freedom. *"Let the wicked forsake his way, and the unrighteous man his thoughts, and let him return unto the Lord."*

When we realize that prosperity comes not through material means but through the action

of rich ideas in Consciousness, we shall stop
entertaining thoughts and beliefs that oppose
our good. We shall embody only those thoughts
which we wish to see out-pictured in our lives.

But how do we know that prosperity and
poverty are states of mind? Because every effect is exactly like its cause. If there were no
poverty thoughts, there could be no poverty
conditions. *Cause and effect* is just another
way of saying *thought and condition.* To have
an outer condition, we must first have an inner
concept. *"As a man thinketh in his heart* [on
the inside], *so is he* [on the outside]." Before
a condition can materialize in the objective, it
must first be thought and believed. That is
the law, and that is why the poor man must
tune out of his mind all the depressing and
limiting thoughts that hold him in a state of
depression. He must not only eliminate the
troublesome thoughts and beliefs that are operating in his Consciousness, but he must refuse
lodging to any other thoughts that may oppose
his good.

Is this subject getting tiresome and mo-
notonous to you? Then put the book down and
sit in the silence for a few moments. Rest
yourself and think of nothing in particular.

We repeat ourselves often for the sake of emphasis. We want you to understand that your power to tune in to the good is in direct ratio to your power to tune out the bad.

In metaphysical science, this process is called *denial*. When you stop the thoughts of want from getting into the mind, this saying is fulfilled: *"Thou openest thy hand, and fillest all things living with plenteousness."* The denial (reversal of the thought of lack) comes first. You sweep out the low thoughts in order that the higher ones may take their place. Then you find that your life and environment are enriched and beautified in ways you never dreamed possible. When you overcome the sense of lack in all directions, every thing will fall into its right place—faith to meet fear, love to meet hate, substance to meet lack, understanding to meet ignorance, health to meet sickness, peace to meet discord, and power to solve every problem. *"Seek ye first the Kingdom of God and His righteousness; and all these things shall be added unto you."*

Some one has said that fear is at the root of all our financial difficulties. Why? Because fear is more commonly associated with lack than any other one thing and because it is a very powerful emotion. By fearing poverty, we give it power to operate in our lives. Listen to some of the common expressions of those who are most often in financial difficulties: "I am afraid I can't afford it." "I am afraid to spend that much." "I am afraid to take a chance." "I am afraid to invest." "I am afraid to trust him." "I am afraid that I won't have the money when the note is due." Those who speak these words are looking to man instead of to God. Now hold that for a moment and try to see the gap which a thought of this kind creates in your consciousness.

Thoughts, whether good or bad, are powerful magnets that build into your life the very idea embodied within them. You are *afraid* that you won't have the money when the note is due; so the Law works in harmony with your fear (feeling) and sees that you do not get it. Did the delay come through the Power or through you? Through you, of course. You asked for the delay with your fear. What you should have done under the circumstances was to have reversed the thought and to have assumed that the money would be there when it was needed. This is the first step in tuning out the poor thoughts that are opposing your good.

Now let us think of the things that must be tuned out of our lives before our reception of the good is perfected. What are they? They are the small thoughts, fears, taboos, failures, disappointments, inhibitions, superstitions, uncertainties, doubts, despairs, forebodings, prohibitions; they are the hurts, insults, injuries, criticisms, self-pityings, self-condemnations— the remembered wrongs of the past.

Up to this point, we have concerned ourselves chiefly with diagnosis or a statement of the problem. Now we shall turn to the therapy or method of operation.

There are two ways of tuning out these mental negatives. One is by vocal renunciation, or by talking them out of ourselves; the other way is by reversing them and mentally withdrawing attention and power from them.

When you vocally renounce the negative factors in your life, it is a good idea to stand before the mirror when you are alone and can talk aloud to the image you see reflected there. Speak out every captive belief that has held you in bondage. Put into words the superficial, immaterial, and unwholesome beliefs that clutter your life. Go down into the subconscious and take yourself apart. Uncover all the inhibitions, false economies, hatreds, jealousies, doubts, discouragements, disappointments, inferiorities, failures, strangling attitudes, and frugal practices. Face your parsimonious, pinched thoughts, your narrow vision, your cramped outlook, and your poverty-stricken environment. Recognize your paralyzing, pinching, cheeseparing habits, shriveling stinginess, and rainy day pressures. Then tune them all out of your life. Tune out every idea of cheapness—cheap clothes, cheap furniture, cheap food, cheap environment, and see yourself living prosperously as God intended you to live.

Do you recognize your emotional complexes, depressions, repressions, and inhibitions for what they are? Acknowledge them and tune them out. Mentally reject these false beliefs until you are absolutely free of them. It makes no difference how much you know about metaphysics nor how many affirmations you have memorized, you will continue to suffer until you tune out the mental causes of your suffering. Jesus said, *"Be not overcome with evil but overcome evil with good."* Prepare your mind for the reception of good by first tuning

out the evil. Make your confession before the
mirror just as though you were talking face
to face with God. Keep talking until you have
uncovered and phrased every disturbing thing
in your life. Let the words flow until all the
negation has poured out.

Begin your heart-to-heart talks by using
such statements as these:

> I now demolish all the discordant and
> untrue records in my subconscious mind.
> They shall return to the dust heap of
> their native state of nothingness. I will
> be done once and for all with the past
> negatives of my life; they must pass!
> I appeal to Infinite Spirit to open my
> mouth and to deliver me of all the old
> foulness, pestering sores, burdensome loads
> that have weighted me down these past
> years, to bring me release and relief, and
> to lead me *"beside the still waters."*

You may have to have these heart-to-heart
talks with yourself many times because of the
persistence of negative thoughts, feelings, and
suggestions. They are bound to return, but
you are not bound to accept them. You can

always think away from them, can always
reverse them. You can expel them just as easily
as you shake the dandruff from your coat collar.
Just make them of no-importance. Treat them
with indifference and unconcern. Challenge
each one with the command of Jesus, *"Get thee
behind me, Satan."* When an unwanted
thought or suggestion comes, reverse it (tune it
out) by putting an opposite desirable thought
in its place.

You recall that St. Paul said, *"Wherefore
seeing we also are compassed about with so
great a cloud of witnesses, let us lay aside every
weight, and the sin which doth beset us, and
let us run with patience the race that is set
before us."*

The second method is based on the same
principle as the first, and both go back to the
process used in changing a basic thought. It
is merely a matter of substituting a good pattern for a bad one.

ASSIGNMENT 1

Go through your Consciousness and make a
list of all the things, events, circumstances, and
experiences that you think may be responsible

for your present state of finances. List all the things that have been troubling you—the position you lost, the deal that failed, the mistakes you have made, the small concepts you have been holding, the mental burdens you have been carrying, and the malignant thoughts that have been festering in your mind; bring them up from the cellar and expose them to the light. It may take you a week or ten days to drag all this rubbish out, but keep on until you get it all. Keep on until there is no hidden thought or belief that can in any way oppose or neutralize your good.

Put each one down on your list and resolve that you will never contemplate it again. If you have been in the habit of discussing financial difficulties, hard times, economic disaster, or depressions with your family or friends, put that practice down. Resolve that you will never do it again. Resolve that you will never think or discuss limitation in any form. If others persist in discussing these things, resolve that you will not listen to them. If you have been in the habit of bemoaning the "good old days" or the difficulties of your present economies, put that habit down. Put down the little luxuries and gratifications that you have been denying

yourself. Put down the things that you persistently say that you cannot afford. List the
bills you owe.

Drag out all the old inhibitions of your
youth. The *I cant's*—the *Dont's*—the *Look
out's*—the *If's*—and the *But's*. Replace them
with the positive, "I can," "I will," "I know,"
"I have." Quit kicking, criticizing, complain-
ing, and finding fault with people and things
around you, and find something to praise. Stop
frowning and scowling, and start smiling at
every one. Destroy everything around you that
suggests poverty or lack. If you are impatient,
list that fault. Be at peace with yourself and
with all men. If you have been thinking meanly
of yourself, list that error and do something
about it. If you have objectionable personal
habits, clean them up. Cleanliness gives you a
luxurious feeling and helps you to radiate prosperity. If there is no demand for you, create
one by getting closer to God. If your eyes
have been seeing limited, unhealthy, and poverty-stricken conditions, train them to see only
the healthy, rich, and prosperous things of life.
Keep on digging and analyzing until you have
ferreted out every enemy thought in your mind.

ASSIGNMENT 2

Now take another sheet of paper and make an inventory of all your possessions such as your house, car, clothing, furniture, jewelry, savings account, bonds, and insurance. Let the material value of these things sink deeply into your mind. Revel in the prosperous feeling they give you.

Insurance companies place a monetary value on eyes, arms, legs, and even fingers. If you totaled your physical assets on the standard compensation of insurance companies only, you would be amazed at how valuable you are. Would you take a million dollars for your two legs, your arms, or your eyes? Would you exchange fresh water and food for all the money in the world? Don't you see how rich you are already? Stop right now and ask yourself, "What am I worried and fearful about?"

ASSIGNMENT 3

Now make a list, comprising (1) all the things that are wrong in your life at the moment and (2) all the things that are right. Do you know what you will find? You will find that things are about ninety per cent right and ten per cent wrong. Then, why all the worry and distress? Why all the stomach ulcers and nerves? Because you are dwelling on the ten per cent that are wrong and are ignoring the ninety per cent that are right. How will you break this bondage? By acting, of course, with the ninety per cent that are right. You will begin to think and act richly. Instead of wearing cheap clothes, you will buy good ones. Instead of keeping the good silver and dishes for company, you will use them for the family. Instead of looking for the price of an article, you will look for what you want. Instead of looking for quantity, you will look for quality. If you can have only one dress or suit at a time, you will buy the best. You will think and speak constructively and positively instead of destructively and negatively. You will talk about what you have instead of what you do not have. You will dwell upon the good and substantial things happening in the world and ignore the bad and demoralizing things.

ASSIGNMENT 4

Now that you have made your list, you are ready to tune the poor thoughts and beliefs out of your Consciousness. A *poor* thought is what we have referred to as a soft spot or gap in Consciousness. As long as this gap remains, the condition which it represents will continue to manifest in the outer world. Our first step, therefore, is to close this gap from the inside. If the only existence poverty has is in the thoughts of man, to withdraw the belief in poverty is to destroy the poverty. Solomon said practically the same thing in these words: *"Keep thy heart* [Consciousness] *with all diligence for out of the heart are the issues* [circumstances, conditions, and experiences] *of life."* This is a wonderful thought, for it means that there is no poverty, want, or depression in your life that is not maintained by your own thinking. In other words, there is no failure in your purse, bank account, business, or affairs; the whole basis for every loss, failure, or bankruptcy is in your Consciousness. It is clear, therefore, that by taking possession of your Consciousness, you can tune out all that is ugly, frustrating, and poor and can tune in all that is beautiful, satisfying, and rich.

The proper way to handle a fear thought (which is a common cause of poverty) is to cut it off before it has had a chance to complete itself in your mind. In other words, get the

thought before it gets you. "I am afraid—."
Cut it off there, and use a positive firm denial
such as this: "It is a lie. *'The Lord is my Shepherd; I shall not want.'* Everything I need is
now in instant manifestation. *'The earth is the
Lord's and the fulness thereof.'* *'The silver is
mine, and the gold is mine, saith the Lord of
hosts.'* *'. . . every beast of the forest is mine,
and the cattle upon a thousand hills.'* *'All that
I have is thine.'*—*Now* does the Spirit of all
Good that lives within supply me with every
need."

If you are one of the persons who find
that physical action reenforces their mental
effort, write the offending thought down on
a piece of paper and drop it quickly into
a little box that you have provided for
that purpose. The idea back of this plan
is to lock the baleful thoughts up so that
they can't get out to bother you again. Put
them under lock and key; this dramatization
helps to convince the mind that you are through
with them. If you date them, you will be able
to see how long it takes to eliminate the offending thought.

In the beginning, you may have to make
a record fifty or a hundred times a day, but the

process will have the same effect upon the troublesome thought as repeated rejection would have upon an unwelcome visitor at your door. If you keep turning him away with a firm denial, he will finally give up and stop bothering you. Of course, some students will prefer to visualize this process instead of dramatizing it. No matter which method you use, if there is no response in your thought to the thoughts that oppose your good, they will eventually drop away. When they drop away, you are out of your difficulties.

ASSIGNMENT 5

Now that you have isolated your poor thoughts, or have them safely locked in your little box, you are ready for your next assignment. For the next week, beginning today, I want you to do the following things:

1. Keep all your troubles and problems locked up tight. Keep yourself in a relaxed state of mind for that period and refuse to think about them.

2. Avoid speaking one word of negation, criticism, trouble, lack, meanness, depression, doubt, fear, or discouragement to any one.

3. Think prosperity, believe prosperity, talk prosperity, act prosperity, feel prosperity. Be prosperous, look prosperous, and live prosperously. In fact, do everything prosperously, just as though you were the richest person in the world.

I know this may seem ridiculous when perhaps you haven't enough money to pay the gas bill, but you must take a radical stand if you are going to succeed. Remember you are dealing with an invisible Substance which, although not conscious of your troubles, is waiting to shape itself around your thoughts and bring into your life the things about which you are thinking. That is why it is so important to keep your mind off your troubles and on God.

The vital thing, as you can see, is never under any circumstances to permit yourself to contemplate a thought of want. If poverty and prosperity are states of mind, you make your own depression. You make it by your own small imperfect thoughts about God and yourself. When you have tuned out the poverty thoughts, you will find that the poverty conditions have automatically disappeared.

CHAPTER 7

TUNING IN

Up to this point we have been largely concerned with the science of Prosperity. Now we shall concentrate on the technique or mechanics of demonstration. If you have thoroughly digested the preliminary instructions and conditioned your mind, the tuning-in to your good will be easy. To demonstrate prosperity is no more difficult than to tune in to a certain wave length or station on your radio. Make a perfect contact, and you get a perfect result. Make an imperfect contact, and you get distortion.

There are three things necessary for tuning in to what you want:

1. A clearly formulated idea.

2. A word pattern to impress it upon the subconscious mind.

3. Faith to keep the idea growing.

"If thou canst believe, all things are possible to him that believeth." Every one of these elements is necessary to a perfect demonstration,

but the most important of the three is FAITH. Faith acts upon all the forces of the universe to materialize the images we believe in. God made *"Every plant of the field before it was in the earth, and every herb of the field before it grew."* So we must make (must image) our desires before they can be fulfilled. In the beginning of everything was the Word, or mental image. First must come the mental image— a clearly formulated idea; second, the affirmation telling the subconscious that the thing imaged is already yours; third, faith to speed up the Law of Attraction. Follow this pattern, and your thoughts will become things, and your desires will be fulfilled. See clearly the thing you want, give it the power of your faith, and all the forces of the universe will rush in to give it form.

"The source and center of all man's creative power," says Glenn Clark, "the power that above all others lifts him above the level of brute creation and that gives him dominion, is his power of making images, or the power of the imagination." Under the image, however, we must put the foundation of faith. *"Faith is the substance of things hoped for,*

the evidence of things not seen." Faith activates our good; the moment unfaith creeps in,
the image is destroyed.

Baudouin said, "To be ambitious for wealth
and yet always expecting to be poor; to be always doubting your ability to get what you
long for, is like trying to reach east by traveling west. There is no philosophy that will
help a man to succeed when he is always doubting his ability to do so, and thus attracting
failure.

"You will go in the direction in which you
face. There is a saying that every time the
sheep bleats, it loses a mouthful of hay. Every
time you allow yourself to complain of your
lot, to say—'I am poor; I can never do what
others do; I shall never be rich; I have not the
ability that others have,' you are laying up so
much trouble for yourself.

"No matter how hard you may work for
success, if your thought is saturated with the
fear of failure, it will kill your efforts, neutralize your endeavors, and make success impossible."

We must, therefore, condition our minds to
receive the thing that we have imaged. The

law cannot do anything for us unless we move with it. We are surrounded by the limitless, inexhaustible, all-providing Power of God, but it can be to us only what we believe it to be. It is around us in the same way that the radio waves are all around us and within us. God, perfection, healing, power, money, position— everything that we can possibly desire is at this moment in our being. We can listen or not listen, but these things do not go away because we are not listening to them. All of these things are in God, and God's impetus is fulfillment. He wants us to have the money we have been trying to get, the home we have been longing for, the automobile we have been looking at, the position we have been talking about. We feel these things and want them *because God is wanting them through us.*

Now we come to that marvelous declaration of Jesus: *"The Kingdom of God is within you."* It is within you (in the entire universe) in the same way that the radio waves are within you. It is within you as a potential, as the oak is within the acorn, as the lily is within the bulb. The Kingdom of God is the Life Principle of all form. It is Omniscient, Omnipresent, and Omnipotent. It is within your

Consciousness waiting to be activated; it is there as everlasting life, power, prosperity, peace, and happiness. We stop or change the action of this Life Principle, and failure follows in our bodies or in our affairs.

Robert Collier says: "Life is intelligent. Life is all-powerful. And Life is always and everywhere seeking expression. What is more, Life is never satisfied. It is constantly seeking greater and fuller expression. The moment you stop expressing more and more of life, that moment life starts looking around for other and better outlets.

"The only thing that can restrict Life is the channel through which it works. The only limitation upon it is the limitation you put upon it.

"In other words, you are not trying to get something that God doesn't want you to have when you set out on the pathway of a full prosperity. You are simply conforming to the Law of His expression in and through you as prosperity—you are opening the way for God to reach out through you into all your life, and into the lives of those about you, and show forth His Divine Abundance of 'Every good and every perfect gift.' "

Here you are, trying to find a way out of your cramped conditions, and all the while there is this unlimited, immeasurable, unfathomable, exhaustless flow of promise trying to get into your life. What are you going to do with your knowledge? Are you going to by-pass it as a beautiful theory, or are you going to condition your mind to receive the gift? Perhaps you are critical, doubtful, fearful, intolerant, greedy, selfish, or unkind, and have shut off your supply. You may have stopped your good so that it is now stagnating within you. Do you dislike or hate someone? The All-Providing Power cannot flow through you while you hate, and the mighty gift that awaits you cannot materialize.

Jesus said: *"No man can serve two masters. . . . Ye cannot serve God and mammon."* You must have a Consciousness of one kind. You must be one-pointed. You must see with the single eye. You must think with the Mind of Christ. Now ask yourself these questions: Can a bottle contain undiluted water and undiluted ink at the same time? Can you be in the light and in the darkness at the same time? Can you be conscious and unconscious at the same time? Can you think two thoughts at the same time?

"Do men gather grapes of thorns or figs of thistles?" Is that what you have been trying to do with your life, with your thinking? Have you been trying to follow two ideas and get one result? If you have, you must get a clear realization of the Principle involved and get a new relationship to it. Negative conditions are simply positive conditions in reverse; poverty is simply prosperity turned up side down.

SUMMARY OF PRINCIPLES OF DEMON-STRATING PROSPERITY

1. The purpose of this book is to plant the idea of prosperity so deeply in your subconscious mind that it will produce definite and concrete results in your life. This result can be accomplished by the direct and immediate use of your conscious mind.

2. The starting point is the Practice of the Presence of God. You will do everything (thinking, speaking, acting, praying, working) as though you were actually in God's Presence and as though He were doing these things through you.

3. Practicing the Presence of God merely consists of keeping God in the forefront of

your Consciousness as much of the time as you can and of associating Him with every activity in your life. Practicing the Presence is the key to spiritual demonstration.

4. When you have a problem, bring it into the Presence and ask God to solve it for you. Do not struggle with the problem or turn it over in your mind, but place it lovingly, gently, and quietly in His hands. Simply maintain your awareness of the Presence, and behold your problem in detachment and peace as you would view a beautiful sunset or scene. This is the Law of Laborless Activity (reversed effort). You have nothing more to do; you have brought the All-Providing Power of God to bear upon your needs. Your problem will be solved from within. That which is hidden will be revealed. That which is lacking will be supplied. Laborless activity is demonstration reduced to the simplicity of Power.

5. The next step is to free yourself from human thinking and material attachments. If all lack, limitation, and impoverishment stem from the human mind (the mind of

the flesh), to leave that mind (to allow it to fall into disuse) is to leave the limitation, struggle, and stress. Be sure that you do not use personal effort or force in any way. Let everything be done for you by letting everything be done through you.

6. If you turn within for the fulfillment of your needs, you will succeed.

7. The only effort required in metaphysical practice is to reach a certain state of Consciousness, or attitude of mind.

8. *"With all thy getting, get understanding."* Understanding is sufficient for every need. If you have it, you need nothing else. It will accomplish everything that needs to be done.

9. To bring any desire into the Presence is to fulfill it. To bring any illness into the Presence is to heal it. To bring any problem into the Presence is to solve it.

10. If you would demonstrate abundance, do not identify yourself with lack, but Practice the Presence of God by seeing abundance everywhere and in everything.

11. Practice the Presence of God until every failure becomes a success.

12. If your desire is not fulfilled, it is because you are unconsciously denying it by
fear, doubt, or worry.

13. To demonstrate a full, continuous, and
irrevocable supply, you must turn from the
carnal mind (decadent, stagnant, and
static) to the Christ Mind (active, alive,
and creative).

14. The human (carnal) mind believes that
forms (tangible things) are outside of Consciousness. It believes that circumstances are
greater than God and that matter is more
real than Spirit. Under that belief, man
becomes the servant of matter (circumstances and conditions) instead of its
master. The carnal-minded man is what
the world call a materialist. Having the
principle in reverse, he is not only opposing (acting against) God, but he is acting
against himself. One metaphysician has
referred to this type of thinking as "mortal

mind" thinking, which is, of course, equivalent to no thinking at all. Let us remember that we cannot draw a sharp line
between matter and spirit without separat-
ing ourselves from Good. Matter is Mind
in extension, or Spirit in form.

15. Consciousness is both the center and the circumference of everything in our lives. It is continually attracting or repelling something.

16. Since this is a mental world, everything in it can be brought into our Consciousness. Ernest Holmes says, "In our mental treatments for prosperity, we resolve things into ideas, conditions into states of thought, and act upon the premise that the thought is the father of the thing. This method is both direct and effective, and when rightly used becomes a law unto the thing thought of."

17. Everything in your life (the good and the not-good) depends upon your Consciousness. Change your Consciousness, and you change your world.

18. Christ Consciousness (which includes all things) is realized through right thinking. Undesirable trends of thought can be changed by thought control. When the mind has been divested of negative habits, its tendency is to heal automatically. The right point of view will meet any need.

19. Your responsibility is to know the Truth and to think in God's Presence. The power of your word is in your Consciousness.

20. Since there is no law of poverty, there is no excuse for being poor.

21. When the thought of prosperity is firmly fixed in Consciousness, its manifestation is certain.

22. When the proper pattern (conducting medium) has been provided, abundance will flow through your Consciousness and manifest itself in your affairs.

23. The prosperity which you affirm must be supported by a rich Consciousness.

24. The prosperity that you seek is seeking you. It will be manifested (out-pictured) according to the riches of your mind.

25. Maintain the eye of expectancy. The more you expect, the more your Consciousness will attract.

26. You must know with your whole mind that there is no obstruction to the operation of the Law of Prosperity in your life.

27. To keep matter and spirit together is to act with God.

28. When your word acts creatively, it is not because you have made it creative but have allowed God to act through it.

29. The four parts in demonstration are these: (1) Making your claim. (2) Accepting what you have claimed. (3) Realizing the peace that comes from the consciousness of fulfillment. (4) The materialization or outward manifestation of that which has been embodied within the thought.

30. *"He that hath a bountiful eye shall be blessed."* To fulfill the law of prosperity, see all things with the prosperous eye.

CHAPTER 8

MIND MODELS

For many years, it has been our custom at The Shrine of the Healing Presence to furnish each person attending the Sunday morning services with what we call a *Mind Model* to be used during the following week. These are little cards containing positive creative affirmations to be repeated until they sink deep into the subconscious mind. They are spiritual slogans, so to speak, for the purpose of healing and integrating body, mind, and affairs. When a thought becomes habitual or subjective, it forms in us a consciousness of itself. It becomes an inner conviction or pattern through which the law works. Man creates nothing but the form and mold.

Any one can demonstrate prosperity who believes that he can and who will take the trouble to put rich ideas to work through the Law. Universal Substance is neutral, plastic, and impressionable. It will take any form that our thoughts and feelings give it. It doesn't know positive or negative, prosperous or poverty thoughts. Jesus said, *"As thou hast believed, so be it done unto thee."* If you are in bondage to poverty thoughts, you cannot hope to express prosperous conditions. If you habitually think opulent thoughts, you will find prosperity on the material plane.

Many persons blame economic disturbances and heredity (prenatal influences) for the adverse and impoverished conditions in their lives. Mr. A. says that his parents, grandparents, and great grandparents have always been poor. Mr. B. says that he was born during the panic of ninety-three and that he has never been able to overcome it. Mr. C. says that his money-making powers were definitely crippled during the depression of twenty-nine. We all suffer more or less from the adverse influences and negative beliefs of others, but there is no reason why any one of us should remain in these grooves of experience. If every man has immediate access to the Source of Supply in his Consciousness, there is no reason why anyone should remain poor.

In metaphysical science, we change the unwanted condition by changing our attitude toward it and by changing our Consciousness. We change the offending and troublesome patterns (1) by a definite conviction that they can no longer operate through us and (2) by substituting better and more productive patterns. Thoughts of abundance will always reverse thoughts of limitation. The Principle is that whatever sinks into the subconscious mind will be out-pictured in our experience. Thoughts of abundance act as a magnet to draw into our lives the rich blessings of God.

But let us remember that thought is both causative and creative. *"In the beginning was the Word, and the Word was with God, and the Word was God." "All things were made by Him." "In Him was life; and the life was the light of men."* In these three verses, you have the foundation and principle of all spiritual practice. A word is a vehicle or pattern of thought. You do not put power and prosperity into your word; you take it out. St. John is saying that God created all things through the power of the Word and that we, re-enacting the Divine Nature, have the same power in us. If we train ourselves to dwell upon the Abundance of the Unconditioned Power that makes things out of Itself, if we learn to see abundance everywhere and in everything, we shall build opulent and prosperous conditions in our lives.

The secret of attracting what we want from the universe is in our ability to focus our minds upon an idea until it forms in us a consciousness of itself. Not many people can do this, however, because not many people can concentrate on a mental image for any length of time. Fluctuating between the higher and the lower potentials, they are constantly diverted by intrusions, vagaries, fantasies, and the ebb and flow of the mind. Jesus said, *"If thine eye be single* [if thy mind be one-pointed], *thy whole body shall be full of light."*

If our desire is to integrate (synchronize) the conscious and subconscious phases of mind, this one-pointedness is an absolute necessity. The picture of our desire must be clear, dynamic, penetrating, and powerful. It must reach clear down to the point of acceptance, action, and creation. We must press our claim with such convincing tones that the subconscious mind will go to work at once to bring it into being.

Now you can see why we use Mind Models in our work. Once a Mind Model is thoroughly established (embodied in Consciousness), the out-picturing is certain. *"As a man thinketh in his heart, so is he."* What a man has in his subconscious mind demonstrates itself. We cannot prevent thoughts of lack, limitation, and fear from getting into the conscious mind, but we can prevent their crystallizing and hampering our work. We can do it by realizing that our word is the Law of Elimination to every negative and unwanted thought.

On one occasion, Jesus said that *"A good man out of the good treasure of the heart bringeth forth that which is good."* We should remember that when we are building new Mind Models within our Consciousness. To give them sturdy and enduring foundations, we must repeat them many times a day, slowly, calmly, and feelingly. This foundation process may require hundreds of repetitions, or it may require thousands. It makes no difference. The important thing is to keep the channels open (free from obstructions) and to keep the mighty current of God's Power flowing through us. The Mind Model should be our first thought in the morning and our last thought at night. We should live with it, act with it, think with it, speak with it, and sleep with it until the idea takes root and flowers in our lives.

There are many reasons why people fail in spiritual work; the most common one is probably lack of persistence. God withholds nothing from us. To believe that He answers one man's prayer and ignores the prayer of another is to deny His goodness. St. James says: *"Every one that asketh receiveth."* It makes no difference how many times you may have failed or how fruitless your efforts may have been, it is still true that it is done unto you as you believe. It is still true that *"No good thing will He withhold from them that walk uprightly* [that do things in the right way]."

The importance of persistence in spiritual work cannot be overemphasized. Spiritual gifts are the most expensive gifts in the world. Healing is expensive. Righteousness is expensive. Dominion is expensive. Answered prayer is expensive. Prosperity is expensive. In fact, anything worth having is expensive. It is expensive in the tremendous amount of mental and spiritual coin that one must pay for it.

Do you remember the story Jesus told of the importunate widow who was in trouble and needed help? The narrative tells us that she sought out a judge. That was a sensible thing to do because she apparently had no one else to whom she could turn. Widows of her day, however, received little or no consideration.

They were at the mercy of every charlatan and crook, and their fate was often very pitiable. You recall that Jesus denounced the scribes who *"devour widows' houses, and for a pretense make long prayers."*

Jesus painted this picture just as black as He could. The judge was not only a double-dealer but a blasphemer as well. He cared nothing for public opinion; *"he feared neither God nor man."* What could a lone woman do against such a man? She had no money with which to bribe him, and no friends with whom to influence him. There was just one thing that she could do and that was to wear him out. Her weapons were persistence, entreaty, and pleading. She would not take *No* for an answer, and her presence was to him like a thorn in his side. She shadowed him night and day. Wherever the judge went, she went. There was no escape from her.

Finally in desperation, he granted her request, admitting that it was the only way he could get rid of her: *"Though I fear not God, nor regard man; yet because this widow troubleth me, I will avenge her lest by her continual coming she weary me."*

Recall, too, the parable of the friend who responded at midnight to his neighbor's demand for bread *"because of his importunity."*

There are many lessons in these parables; the most important one is the virtue of importunity. Despite God's love, beneficence, and compassion, He will not be moved by weak and half-hearted demands. The power is there, as St. Paul pointed out in the closing of one of the Epistles to the Ephesians: *"Now unto Him that is able to do exceeding abundantly above all that we ask or think, according to the power that worketh in us."* But the power must be invoked by persistency, by seeking, and by whole hearted demands. Jesus commanded us to ask, to seek, and to knock. Do you give up easily? Then change your ways. Give Him no rest until He establishes what you desire. Keep on keeping on.

Make your claim and press it. Work until every *no* becomes a *yes.* If you fail today, start all over again tomorrow. *"In due season, we shall reap if we faint not."*

These parables do not teach that God is reluctant to give us what we ask; they do show, however, that He responds only to the affirmative and persistent attitude of mind. It is the story of Jacob, wrestling with his angel: *"I will not let thee go except thou bless me."* It is the story of Paul, praying over his thorn in the flesh. It is the story of Jesus in the garden: *"His sweat was as it were great drops of blood falling down upon the ground."*

What is Jesus telling us in these parables? He is telling us that it is the all-consuming desire that is fulfilled. It is the spirit-filled prayer that is answered. It is the affirmative Consciousness that attracts the most. If an indifferent and godless judge will avenge a woman because of her importunity, will not a loving Father reward those who press their claim?

Why, then, do we get so discouraged over our delays? If our faith is weak, it needs to be strengthened. If our attitude is impoverished, it needs to be enriched. If our Consciousness is small, it needs to be enlarged. If our vision is dull, it needs to be sharpened. If our mind is capricious, it needs to be stabilized. If our desire is hazy, it needs to be clarified. If our sights are low, they need to be raised. We must change our position in the Law; we must know that this is a mental world. We must stop watching others to see what they are doing and how they are doing it. But, of course, if our Consciousness were wholly unified with Reality, importunity would be unnecessary. We would demonstrate our good (automatically) by virtue of what we are.

I hope I am not hurrying you with your work, but I am enthusiastic about what you can do. If you know what you want and have a clear picture of your desire, you are now ready to build the new pattern and release it into mind. This action is the most difficult part of the process. Ernest Holmes says, "The thought and the idea must be abandoned into Mind. We have to take hold of the idea, knowing that we are dealing with Reality and let go of the idea knowing that Reality is dealing with it. It is not easy to hold and let go at the same time, and yet in a certain sense that is what we have to do. We are dealing with something that takes ideas and makes facts out of them. As this is understood, the power is set in motion which will manifest at a level which will be absolutely identical with the mental and spiritual level of the embodiment of the idea."

If you were here in person, I could help you build your Mind Model; but you can build it for yourself. Simply take five or six small white cards and print or write your desire on them. Then put the cards in the most conspicuous places in your home, office, or automobile. Many of our men keep one in their bill fold, one on their desk, one on their pillow, and another on the bathroom mirror where they shave. The purpose of the Mind Model cards is two fold: (1) To keep the picture of your desire before you as many hours out of the day as possible, and (2) To keep an active relationship (reciprocal action) between the conscious and subconscious minds at all times.

The subconscious is receptive and suggestible; it embodies new ideas only through repetition, feeling, and realization. It responds only to the strongest and most insistent demands. It is imperative, however, that you follow to the letter the instructions to repeat the affirmation many times a day. When the idea contained on the card is finally integrated with the subconscious mind, it goes to work with all its power to give the idea form. *"And the Word was made flesh and dwelt among us."*

The process is very similar to the process of projecting moving pictures on a screen. When the film (pattern) engages the light, the form comes into expression. That is why repetition, imagination, and realization are so important.

The idea must be registered with such depth of feeling that it engages the activity, life, and power of the Creative Mind. We must contemplate it and dwell upon it until it becomes our primary or basic thought. We must hold it in place until every faculty and power are working toward that end. We must drive the nail to its very head. The first blow (visualization) sets the direction of the nail, but it is only by repeated blows that it is driven to its goal.

Victor Hugo said: "Nothing is so powerful in the world as an idea whose time has come." No man has ever become rich unless he has been used by a rich idea. We are all used by ideas; the unfortunate thing is that most of us allow ourselves to be used by wrong ideas. Outside forces are not to blame for ills and woes; spurious and fallacious thoughts are to blame. We are afraid of rich, abundant, and opulent ideas; we are afraid to give ourselves to a great idea and make it our own.

When we have whole-heartedly accepted a desirable idea, have made it our own, have let it become an integral part of us, we are ready for the manifestation to come into being. The importance of our choice of ideas is apparent. Joshua called upon the tribes of Israel to *"Choose ye this day whom ye will serve* [choose the kind of ideas that you are going to express]."

Now that we have an understanding of how the Law works, let us take a practical example. Since by your reading of this book, you admit your need, we can assume that the definite specific desire which you have put into words and placed on cards is associated with Prosperity. Having faced your need, you must convince yourself that what you need is already here. Is there plenty of money in the world? Do you know any one who has plenty? Then get the feeling of it. If any one else has plenty, you can have plenty too. *"God is no respecter of persons."* The Law is impersonal. *"He maketh His sun to shine upon the evil and on the good, and sendeth rain on the just and on the unjust."* What has come to other persons can come to you.

You have by this time met and answered two questions: 1. What is my need? 2. Can I share in Prosperity?

The third question naturally is, "How can I get this Prosperity?" You can get it in the only way that any one else gets things—through the action of the Law of Consciousness. Ask yourself if there is anything outside of Consciousness except that which you put outside Consciousness.

I like this illustration, given by J. Lowrey Fendrich, Jr: "Why is it that I can walk or lift my hand? Because I know I can. If I didn't know I could, I couldn't. The proof could be established in five minutes. I have two strong legs. I can see and I have a sense of balance. I try to walk on a steel girder a few flights above the earth. I cannot walk. But I still have the same two legs, still have a sense of balance. Why? Because in consciousness I have reversed my ability to walk. Now I am frightened—now I am anxious—now I am worried."

Do you see why we fall over into the realm of the undesirable—into lack and limitation? It is because we believe that we are limited. We alibi in some such fashion as this: "My forebears have always had menial jobs." "My mother took in washing." "My father was a waiter, and my grandfather was a janitor." "My brother is a barber, and I am a clerk in a store." "No one in my family has ever been able to keep money after he gets it." Isn't it amazing what we do to ourselves? We shut ourselves off as an isolated sentence from the Book of Life. We tell ourselves that we can't have this or that; and, of course, we don't get it.

Your last question must always be this: Is this desire of mine spiritually legal? Is it God's will that I should have plenty? Let the Scripture answer:

"What things soever ye desire, when ye pray, believe that ye have received them, and ye shall have them."

"My God shall supply all your need according to His riches in glory by Christ Jesus."

"God is able to make all grace abound toward you; that ye, always having all sufficiency in ALL THINGS, may abound to every good work."

"They shall prosper that love Thee. Peace be within thy walls, and prosperity within thy palaces."

"Let the Lord be magnified which hath pleasure in the prosperity of his servant."

"The blessing of the Lord, it maketh rich, and He addeth no sorrow with it."

'And all things, whatsoever ye shall ask in prayer, believing, ye shall receive."

Now for a few minutes turn back to the Mind Model given to you on the first page: I AM PROSPERITY. Contemplate this thing we call *Prosperity.* How can you register this idea in the subconscious mind so that it will become the inevitable expression of your every waking moment? How will you visualize prosperity? You visualize prosperity just as you do anything else. Prosperity is a state of being; to experience it you must appropriate it. Now I am going to put the proposition squarely up to you: How would you feel and act if *right now* you had everything you wanted? See yourself acting in that way; capture the feeling of completeness and satisfaction that you would have. Luxuriate in the thought. Prosperity starts in the mind as an idea, and then comes out into form. First, the mental Principle, then the pattern (impressing the thought upon the subconscious mind which acts creatively and intelligently upon it), and then the expression: these are the steps in the process. You give the order (you provide the matrix or form); God fills it. Does this sound unfamiliar? Then listen to St. Paul: *"I have planted, Apollos watered, and God gave the increase."*

Now take your idea into the Silence; repeat it meditatively and thoughtfully many times. Relax from head to foot; get the emotional impact of the idea. Keep yourself consciously in God's Presence, and state your desire. Bring God, yourself, and your desire together in Consciousness. You have not only set the Law in motion, but you have developed a new point of view. God's gifts are already in instant manifestation. There is no desire that you can possibly have that is not already fulfilled. For every demand, there is supply. For every desire, there is fulfillment. Just as you adjust your radio to certain programs on the air, you adjust your mind to the fulfillment of certain desires in your life. You do not bring the programs into your home, but you tune in to programs that are already there. So, you consciously and deliberately tune in to the Law of Plenty.

The next step is to identify yourself with the object of your desire. If it is true of God, it is true of you. Know this; make sure that you are not admitting any thought (past or present) that will in any way restrict or limit the expression of your good. If you are entertaining such a thought, you are causing the

Power to work through that limiting condition, and are consequently delaying your demonstration. Jesus said in effect, "Seek spiritual riches first, and material riches will be added unto you." The prosperity you affirm must be supported by a rich Consciousness.

MEDITATIONS ON PROSPERITY

STEP I

Use one or all of the Meditations that follow. Feel the substance of each declaration in every part of your being. Say the words quietly and meditatively and with convincing tones.

I AM PROSPERITY

Prosperity is the law of my life.

This Law is continuously operative in my affairs.

I now open my mind, body, purse, business, and all else in order that this prosperity may flow through me in abundant measure.

I am confident that I shall have plenty to meet every need when it is due.

My income is in the keeping of Infinite Wisdom.

My affairs are guided by Divine Intelligence.

I AM PROSPERITY

There is no delay and no obstruction to the operation of this Mind Model.

There is no confusion, contradiction, inhibition, doubt, or limiting factor of any kind associated with it.

"ALL THAT THE FATHER HATH" IS MINE NOW.

Prosperity flows through me in an uninterrupted stream, eliminating everything unlike itself.

There is nothing in me that can obstruct, congest, or retard my Supply in any way.

I am forever one with the Infinite Supply of God. It knows me, claims me, and rushes to me.

I accept this Supply for myself and for everyone who is in need.

I AM PROSPERITY

My Supply is wherever I am.
It comes to me from every direction.

I accept this abundance, bounty, and opulence today.

I know that It is externalizing itself in my life and affairs.

I AM PROSPERITY

I am not concerned about the limitations and fears of yesterday.

I know that right now everything is made rich.

I let go of all my injurious habits of thought, my foolish actions, and my tendency to failure.

I separate my thought from any belief in want, incapacity, and inability.

I disclaim the idea that I am broke, despondent, poor, crushed, defeated, or dependent.

New opportunities are now opening to me.

All financial obligations, debts, and pressures are being liquidated.

All tension is being released.

All unhappy circumstances, conditions, and misunderstandings are being harmonized.

Wherever I go, I shall meet prosperous people and prosperous conditions.

Whenever I think, I shall think with joy, optimism, happiness, and peace.

Whatever I do, I shall do with wisdom, authority, power, and right action.

My whole Consciousness accepts these truths. I am made rich!

I AM PROSPERITY

Today I enter into the Consciousness of abundance and plenty.

I know that this Mind Model is already established in me, and I thank God for its fulfillment.

I know that everything I do will prosper.

I know that every demand I make upon the Universe will be honored.

I expect success in all my undertakings.

I am demonstrating prosperity because there is nothing in me to deny it.

I let blessings, money, and possessions flow into me from every direction.

I see abundance everywhere I look.

I am opening my mind to a larger influx.

I believe that the Law of Prosperity operating through me will bless and enrich everyone I meet.

STEP II

Now think of the object of your specific, individual Mind Model and say:

> I know that the Spirit of God working in and through me is now operating upon my desire. *"My word shall not return unto me void, but it shall . . . prosper in the thing whereto I sent it."* I know that I now have the prosperity which I affirm. I know that everything in my experience is working together to bring this about.

Feel these patterns deeply, feel them with power. Feel them with happiness and conviction. Let them dig deeply into your emotional nervous system. Praise them. Give thanks for them. Thrill to them. Speak your word with convincing tones. Call it with energy and devotion.

STEP III

Remembering Emerson's statement that "A prayer for less than the all good is vicious," make these declarations for every one who is in need:

> O Thou Divine Fountain of Life in its fulness, Thou who hast put Thy Holy Spirit in me to guide me in the way of Prosperity and Peace, I pray to Thee on behalf of those throughout the world who suffer because of lack, want, poverty, hunger, and sickness. Awaken them to a knowledge that Thou art now with them —a Mighty Power by whose Hand their every need may be supplied.

> Enable them to know that they may be led out of every danger into ways of Peace and Plenty if they will but put their trust in Thee, for *"They that seek the Lord shall not want any good thing."*

And to the suffering millions send out this word from the center of your being, not in your own strength but in the Strength of God, not in your own name but in the Name of Jesus Christ:

> The Lord Thy God in the midst of thee is mighty to save from poverty, and hunger, and from every other evil thing. If you will but put your trust in Him, He will call to your aid that which will meet your need. He will give you His Prosperity and Peace.

> In the Name and by the Power of Jesus Christ. Amen.

STEP IV

At this stage in your Meditation, you are ready to let fall your Mind Models. By that, we mean that you are to put them aside for ten or fifteen minutes and take no thought about them. This is the gestation period. You have made your claim; now you are going to think of nothing but God.

Center your whole thought on such statements as these: *"I AND THE FATHER ARE ONE."* Feel it. Glory in it. *"Your heavenly Father knoweth what things ye have need of."* Know that you are *"like a tree planted by the*

*rivers of water" whose "leaf shall not wither:
and whatsoever he doeth shall prosper."*
Realize that Omnipresent Substance is waiting to be released into every area of your
life; put everything else out of your mind.
*"I am God, and beside me there is none
else."* Work for absolute serenity, quiet,
and peace. Feel God's Power moving through
you. *"I can of mine own self do nothing."*
*"The Father that dwelleth in me He doeth the
works."*

Repeat the Twenty-Third Psalm or any
Scriptural passages that induce peace and quiet.

You are now at rest; as you continue in your
work, you will find yourself in God's Presence.
You will enter the Peace that passeth all understanding; you will know that your need has
been met. Your demand and God's Supply are
now one. In perfect union with God, there is
no lack. The circuit has been completed; your
desire has been fulfilled. Know that the answer has come. Plan your action as though it
had; then act upon the plan.

Keep the idea, I AM PROSPERITY, flowing through your mind, but do not tell anybody what you are doing. The admonition of

Jesus, *"See that you tell no man"*, is still the best advice in the world. To tell others what you are doing is to break your connection with the subconscious mind. You not only delay your demonstration; you lessen the possibility of fulfilling your desire. Secrecy is a MUST in your work. Your desire is like steam in a boiler that seeks every avenue of escape until it finds a way out. When you hold your new idea in absolute secrecy, it builds up such a pressure that something must give way. It must continue to expand until it finds a point of expression.

The value of repetition cannot be emphasized too much. It is the constant dropping of water upon a stone. It is the constant repetition of the Mind Model that integrates it with the subconscious mind and materializes the idea.

THE FIVE RULES OF DEMONSTRATION

1. Get a clear picture of your desire.

2. Build your Mind Models, and put them in conspicuous places.

3. Repeat your Mind Model many, many times.

4. Identify yourself with your desire; use your technique not less than twice a day.

5. Maintain absolute secrecy. Do not tell anybody what you are doing.

"The stars come nightly to the sky;
The tidal waves come to the sea.
Nor time, nor space, nor deep, nor high,
Can keep my own away from me." *

* Burroughs, John. *"Waiting."*

Dear Reader,

I take leave of you for the time. If I have been able to help you understand this important subject. I am more than satisfied. It is not easy to assimilate because of the divided and undisciplined mind that we bring to it. *"The wisdom of this world is foolishness with God,"* said St. Paul, realizing how necessary it is to rise above human sagacity to become *en rapport* with the Divine.

You have found that this book is not an Aladdin's Lamp to be rubbed with phenomenal results but is instead a simple statement of the Law of Financial Success—a way of demonstrating prosperity. It was written to show the prosperous man as well as the poor man how to consciously use the Law. The prosperous man can increase his prosperity; the poor man can lose his poverty.

"Behold NOW is the accepted time." If you expect your prosperity in the future, you will never realize it. There is no tomorrow. Heaven's dividends are always paid in the present. Your results are in proportion to the expansion of your consciousness, the clarity of your vision, the invincibility of your purpose,

the power of your faith, the depth of your feeling, the completeness of your acceptance, and the extent of your gratitude.

There is much more that I should like to tell you about the Law of Financial Success and its relation to selling property, increasing business, demonstrating jobs, and cutting down financial worries. There are many other practical helps, metaphysical secrets, and usable techniques that I should like to share with you. That is why I am printing a companion volume to this book under the title: *PUTTING THE PROSPERITY IDEA TO WORK.* It is a series of short studies to give you a practical, usable technique for applying the Law in daily needs.

I urge you who seek the blessing of prosperity to be not weary in well doing, for the gratification that attends upon successful endeavor will surely be yours if you persevere and *"wait upon the Lord."*

God bless you, my friend, and may His richest blessings attend you on your way. You are depending upon Principle for all that you will ever need, and Principle never fails.

Robert A. Russell

ACKNOWLEDGEMENTS

In the making of a book such as this, the author finds himself under obligation to many persons.   There are those who have contributed ideas, and there are others whose words are remembered when their source is forgotten or impossible to identify.   The appreciation of the writer is no less sincere because of the impossibility of making public acknowledgement of their service.

In the brief bibliography that follows, the author wishes to acknowledge with deep gratitude his use of specific quotations of some length.

CHAPTER 1.

Beals, Edward C.—*The Law of Financial Success.*   DeVorss & Co.

CHAPTER 2.

Turner, Mary E. — *Weekly Unity.*   Unity School of Christianity.

Ingraham, E. V.—*Wells of Abundance.*   DeVorss & Co.

CHAPTER 3.

Fillmore, Lowell—*Remember.*   Unity School of Christianity.

CHAPTER 4.

Fox, Emmet—*The Mental Equivalent.*   Unity School of Christianity.

Collier, Robert—*Be Rich.*

CHAPTER 5.

Holmes, Ernest—*It's Up to You.*   Institute of Religious Science.

Chilcott, Rhetta M.—*Weekly Unity.*   Unity School of Christianity.

CHAPTER 7.

Collier, Robert—*Prayer Works.*

CHAPTER 8.

Holmes, Ernest—*Science of Mind.*   Institute of Religious Science.

Burroughs, John—*The World's Great Religious Poetry.*   Macmillan Company.

By the Same Author

Putting the Prosperity Idea to Work _____$2.00

Talk Yourself Out of It _____ 2.25

Talk Yourself Into It _____ 2.25

All Things Made New _____ 2.00

The Quickest Way to Everything Good __ 2.00

Vital Points in Demonstration _____ 2.00

Victory Over Fear and Worry _____ 1.90

You Can Get What You Want If
    You Find It Within Yourself _____ 1.90

Getting Better Results From Spiritual
    Practice _____ 1.25

Receiving What You Ask For _____ 1.25

The Answer Will Come _____ 1.25

The Creative Silence _____ 1.00

Making the Contact _____ 1.25

Let's Face It _____ 1.00

Dry Those Tears _____ 1.00

The Science and Use of Spiritual Power___ .50

Cast Your Net on the Right Side
    of the Ship _____ .50

Go Wash in Jordan _____ .50

Out of the Heavens _____ .50

Behold the Man _____ .35

Lightning Source UK Ltd.
Milton Keynes UK
UKHW01f2054120618
324143UK00001B/128/P